The Propagation of New Zealand Native Plants

Lawrie Metcalf

GODWIT

In some ways this book is a joint effort and I am deeply indebted to Geoff Davidson of Oratia Native Plant Nursery, Auckland; Copper and Keith Hay of Forevergreen Nursery, Tauranga; Anita Catchpole of Otari Native Plant Museum, Wellington; and John Baker of the DoC Home Creek Nursery, Manapouri. Their willingness to share information and experiences has helped to make this book much more valuable than it could otherwise have been. Mike Bradstock of Christchurch very kindly supplied information concerning the propagation of the New Zealand mangrove or manawa. I must also thank Peter Arthur of Touchwood Books for access to reference material. Finally, but by no means least, I am also grateful to my wife for her invaluable assistance.

Photographs in the colour section other than the following were taken by the author: *Coprosma rhamnoides, Coprosma brunnea, Gaultheria antipoda, Astelia fragrans* (Yvonne Cave); *Rhapalostylis sapida, Pittosporum crassifolum, Acaena microphylla, Dacrycarpus dacrydioides, Carmichaelia aligera, Clematis paniculata, Phormium cookianum, Bulbinella rossii, Sophora tetraptera* (Rob Lucas)

A GODWIT BOOK
published by
Random House New Zealand
18 Poland Road, Glenfield, Auckland, New Zealand
First published 1995, reprinted 1997, 2000

ISBN 0 908877 71 4

Cover design: Sarah Maxey
Cover photograph: Fruit of titoki, *Alectryon excelsus* (Yvonne Cave)

Typesetting and production by Kate Greenaway

Printed in Hong Kong

Contents

Introduction

It is hoped that this book will enable more New Zealanders to undertake the propagation of our native plants, not only with a reasonable degree of confidence but also with a high degree of success. While it is aimed mainly at amateur growers, it should also prove useful to professionals.

Too many people try to justify a lack of knowledge by saying that they do not have 'green fingers'. It is true that the so-called 'green-fingered' gardeners seem automatically to do the right thing, but others can easily learn what is required. There is nothing magical about plant propagation; all that is required is common sense and the ability to learn some simple skills. Knowledge comes from experience and is gradually built up with time. The aim of this book has been to combine my own knowledge and experience with that freely given by several other growers so that it is available for the benefit of everyone.

As with any subject, there is always more to be learned. Although I have been growing and studying native plants for many years, when I first commenced the research for this book I soon discovered that there is still a great deal which is not known. I hope that others interested in this topic will be stimulated into experimenting and filling in some of the gaps in our knowledge.

There is a great deal of fun and satisfaction to be gained from propagating your own plants. It can also save a considerable amount of money, particularly when relatively large quantities of plants are required; however, there are a number of other reasons why home gardeners, in particular, may wish to propagate their own native plants.

Caring for the environment and protecting the remaining wild populations of many native plants is more critical than ever before. From shorelines to high alpine regions, many species are under threat from introduced browsing animals, human activities and continuing development resulting in denigration and depletion of habitat areas. For a not inconsiderable number of species the long-term survival of wild populations is by no means assured.

Although disputed by some botanists, cultivation of threatened and endangered plants is now recognised as a valid form of conservation. One of the arguments against it is the fact that clonal selection inevitably occurs; however, that is preferable to the possibility of extinction of the species. Cultivation does allow plants, rare in the wild, to be propagated in quantity. If carried out under suitable guidelines, it also enables the revegetation of appropriate areas to be undertaken.

Unfortunately, when some people become keen on native plants they still resort to collecting established plants from wild sources. It is more sensible to purchase your requirements from a nursery or, even better, to try propagating your own. Wild-collected plants are often slow to become established in the garden, whereas those produced in cultivation are usually more vigorous and establish easily. Virtually anybody can go into the bush or mountains and collect plants, but it takes the skills of a competent horticulturist to maintain them in cultivation.

Collecting seeds, in moderation, from wild sources does not do a great deal of harm and is certainly preferable to digging up whole plants. It is a horticultural axiom that after several generations in cultivation a plant becomes easier to grow and propagate. In general, cuttings should be taken from wild sources only if propagation from seed is not practicable or if there is a special form of a particular plant that may not be true-breeding from seed.

Having said that, it is still necessary to collect plant material from wild sources in order to bring into cultivation forms that are superior to existing clones. One aspect deserving greater attention from plant nurseries is inherent frost-hardiness. Many currently grown clones of native plants were originally collected from lowland localities and are not always as hardy as might be expected. To obtain hardier clones of such species, propagation material should be collected from their altitudinal or southernmost limits; a few nurseries are already commencing to do that.

It is important to remember that a permit is necessary before plant material can be collected from Crown land. Likewise, before collecting on privately owned land permission should be obtained from the owner.

For anybody interested in undertaking some environmental planting, being able to propagate your own plants is a definite bonus. Environmental plantings are usually expensive because of the quantities of plants required and there is the added difficulty that the plant material must be propagated from appropriate sources; normally that means from plants growing in or near the area to be planted. Few nurseries cater for that kind of planting and so it is often necessary to grow your own plants. Usually it is preferable to use seed-raised plants because they provide a genetic diversity not possible from vegetatively propagated plants.

For ornamental plantings there is always a desire to select new or superior forms of any plant. To perpetuate such clones it is usually necessary to propagate them vegetatively. Some native plants hybridise very readily and when seed is collected from a plant growing where it may hybridise with a related species or cultivar some very interesting seedlings are sometimes obtained. The majority may turn out to be of no great merit but there is always the chance that one seedling will have qualities that make it worth keeping.

Some plants produce mutations or branch sports, which may be horticulturally desirable. Usually they must be vegetatively propagated. The purple ake ake (*Dodonaea viscosa* 'Purpurea') is interesting in that it arose as a wild mutant plant which has proved to be true-breeding from seed.

Another of the joys of growing your own plants is being able to give surplus plants to friends, exchange them with other enthusiasts, or supply plants for stalls at school fairs and suchlike.

This book does not aim to provide all of the answers, but it is hoped that it will offer enough information to stimulate readers to learn more and to experiment for themselves. Comments and further information will be gladly received in the hope that future editions can be improved.

Lawrie Metcalf

1
Propagation Structures, Equipment and Materials

PROPAGATION STRUCTURES

Propagation structures can vary from high-technology greenhouses capable of producing thousands of plants to a simple plastic bag enclosing a small pot. Some forms of propagation can be performed outdoors with no special facilities, however for most techniques certain minimum facilities are required.

Simple facilities

A plastic bag and pot are the simplest facilities for raising seedlings or rooting cuttings. Most books recommend inverting the plastic bag over the top of the pot and placing a wire hoop in the pot to prevent the bag from collapsing. I prefer to have the mouth of the plastic bag uppermost and held closed with a rubber band or something similar as it is much easier to inspect the contents; the wire hoop is unnecessary. Except when cuttings require absolute humidity, I prefer not to close the bag tightly but to leave a finger-sized opening. Especially for seed raising, this allows a certain amount of ventilation and can help to prevent problems with fungal diseases. The plastic bag should be kept at room temperature and placed where it receives plenty of light but not direct sunlight as it may become excessively hot within the bag.

Outdoor seed beds

These are probably of most use when large quantities of seed are to be sown. With large-scale commercial operations temporary beds are usually formed in the open ground but on a small scale a permanent bed contained within timber edging is preferable. This allows the bed to be raised above ground level, thus ensuring better drainage. The bed should be a maximum of 1.5 m wide so that it is easily accessible from either side. The soil should be well drained and friable and if necessary incorporate sand and humic material. Provision should also be made for shading, which can be manuka brush, wooden lath covers or shade cloth stretched over a wooden frame or hoops of flexible PVC tubing at least 40–50 cm above the seed bed.

Propagation cases

Various kinds of simple propagation cases can be made from boxes and similar receptacles. The simplest is a box, preferably of treated timber, with drainage holes in the bottom. It should be 25–30 cm deep and covered by polythene film or a sheet of glass. If it is to be used for cuttings alone, about 10 cm of propagating medium can be put in the box and the cuttings inserted directly into it. Polystyrene fruit trays (often obtainable free from supermarkets or greengrocers) make ideal containers if wire hoops are inserted at either end of the tray and covered with polythene film.

Propagation cases can be purchased from some garden centres and horticultural suppliers. They consist of a plastic tray for holding the propagation medium and a transparent rigid cover with two adjustable ventilators on top. An electric heating pad, for placing under the tray, is also available, however the temperature is predetermined and cannot be regulated; in my experience it can be a little high and requires good management to overcome it.

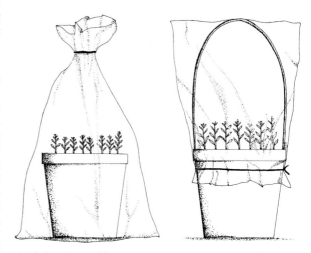

A polythene bag used for rooting cuttings or germinating seed. Left: the pot inside the bag, with the opening held closed by a rubber band; a finger hole is left open for ventilation. Right: the bag inverted over the pot and supported by a wire hoop; the bag is tied around the rim of the pot.

A tray of cuttings enclosed under polythene film supported by wire hoops

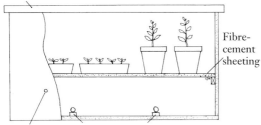

Lid clad with polythene film or glass

Fibre-cement sheeting

Ventilation hole to prevent overheating

Incandescent strip lamps

Detail of a simple heat box to provide bottom heat for rooting cuttings or germinating seed. Drawing not to scale.

A simple way of providing bottom heat for cuttings and seeds is to construct a heat box in which the heat is provided by electric lighting underneath. The light chamber needs to be about 15 cm deep. Incandescent strip lamps (not fluorescent) are preferable to bulbs because the latter tend to concentrate the heat in one area. The division separating the light chamber from the propagating chamber should be made of a non-flammable material such as fibre-cement sheeting. Drill a few ventilation holes in the sides to prevent overheating.

Cold frames

A cold frame may be of any suitable length and for ease of access should not be more than 1.5 m wide. The back should be 45–50 cm high and the front at least 30 cm. Construction materials are normally treated timber, brick, concrete or a heavy grade of fibre-cement sheeting. The lid or 'light' may be covered with glass, PVC, polycarbonate sheeting or clear plastic film. The light can be hinged at the back for easy opening or loosely fitted so that it can be completely removed. Cover the floor with a material that remains moist and helps to maintain a humid atmosphere. Sand, 10 mm stone chips or sawdust are suitable.

Cold frames come in a variety of shapes and sizes and a simple version can be made by constructing a low-level base, about 20 cm high, into which are fixed hoops of steel or flexible PVC pipe covered by plastic film in the form of blinds that can be rolled up. This type is best aligned in a N–S direction. However, cold frames are usually aligned in an E–W direction so that they receive maximum light, although over-heating can be a problem during summer. When used for seed or cutting propagation, shading will be required during very bright conditions.

Heating, usually provided by electrical heating cable laid over the bottom of the frame, enables use of the frame throughout the year and extends the range of plants that can be propagated in it. A probe-type thermostat will be needed to maintain the required temperature.

Small cold frames composed of a metal frame with glass sides and lights are commercially available but their all-glass cladding means they accumulate a great deal of heat and are really only suitable for growing on rather than propagating.

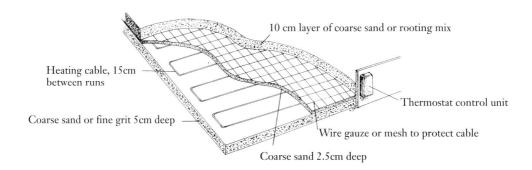

10 cm layer of coarse sand or rooting mix

Heating cable, 15cm between runs

Coarse sand or fine grit 5cm deep

Thermostat control unit

Wire gauze or mesh to protect cable

Coarse sand 2.5cm deep

Layout of a bottom-heating unit using electrical heating cable. Drawing not to scale.

Greenhouses

These vary from the traditional glazed glasshouse to those covered with plastic. A greenhouse may not be any better than a well-constructed and well-managed cold frame but it does enable propagation to be carried out in reasonable comfort and the increased space available also permits a wider range of activities.

Regardless of the construction material, all greenhouses must have good ventilation. Many commercially made greenhouses, particularly tunnel houses, have inadequate air circulation, which can affect plant growth as well as providing ideal conditions for pests and diseases.

Greenhouses used for propagation should be fitted with benches. Not only do they eliminate tiresome bending but the temperature at bench height is decidedly warmer than that at floor level.

Small greenhouses suitable for the home gardener are available as kitsets and are not difficult to assemble. Regardless of whether it is plastic covered or glazed, success will depend on how it is managed. When purchasing a greenhouse, ascertain whether the ventilators provided are adequate for the size of the house and, if necessary, request that extra ventilation be provided.

During bright weather, particularly from late October until about early March, some form of shading may be necessary. Shade cloth is the easiest and most practical means. It is commonly available in grades having shade factors of 30 and 50 percent, although 70 and 80 percent grades are also available. The 50 percent grade is probably suitable for most purposes. It is more effective if used on the outside but this is not always practicable.

Heating can extend the use of the greenhouse, particularly over the winter months, however, it is often impractical to heat small hobby-sized greenhouses. With larger greenhouses it may be more feasible. Electrical heating cable can be used, although it may be rather expensive to run. Lining the greenhouse with polythene film can be a very practical alternative. For the best results there should be a space of 5 cm between the exterior cladding and the polythene lining. Creating a 'double-skinned' greenhouse not only increases the temperature and humidity, it will also protect against light to medium frosts and moderate the effects of severe frosts.

EQUIPMENT AND TOOLS

Propagation containers

Trays, cell trays, punnets, pots and Rootrainers are the main containers required for propagating plants.

Trays are used for seed sowing, pricking out and for rooting cuttings. Plastic trays are preferable as they are lighter to carry, are much easier to keep clean and usually have adequate drainage holes. They also stack or nest together and take up little room in storage. Many plastic trays are only 5 cm deep, which is a little shallow but adequate.

Cell trays (also known as unit containers) are compartmentalised into individual units into which seedlings or cuttings are inserted in a growing medium. With cell trays there is little root disturbance or damage when the plants are potted on. Although used mainly in the commercial field, they could be useful for some home propagators.

Punnets are simply small plastic trays and are primarily used for growing on small seedlings. Many flower and vegetable seedlings are sold in punnets containing 6–12 plants. Home gardeners will find punnets very useful for seed sowing and for handling small quantities of seedlings.

Pots are used for seed sowing, rooting cuttings, potting up young seedlings or rooted cuttings, and for growing on older plants. Nowadays, most pots are made of plastic and are available in a variety of styles and sizes. Plastic pots are light and easily cleaned for re-use. They are also non-porous, which means the medium does not dry out so quickly, but this can be a disadvantage if the propagating medium is not as free-draining as it should be. With age, and especially if they have been outside for long periods, plastic pots become brittle and are easily broken. When purchasing plastic pots, check that the drainage holes are not blocked.

Clay pots are used much less these days except by home gardeners. The main disadvantages of clay pots are their heaviness and that they are easily broken, although with age plastic pots break even more easily. Some modern propagating media will dry out just as quickly in plastic pots as in clay pots. Their use is now confined to one-off purposes such as the growing of specimen plants. I must confess to still having a liking for clay pots even though their use on a large scale is difficult to justify. Their porosity can, however, be an advantage. Cuttings inserted around the outside of a clay pot root more quickly and have better root systems than those placed in the centre of the pot or in a plastic pot. That is because the porous wall of the pot allows greater aeration.

Peat or fibre pots are generally manufactured from peat or mixtures of peat, bark and wood fibres, sometimes with fertilisers incorporated. They are most useful when plants are to be held for only a short time before being potted up or planted out. Being biodegradable, the pot is planted along with the plant and with time will gradually break down, but it is essential they are kept moist otherwise the roots will be unable to penetrate the pot wall. When planting out, the fibre pot should be lightly crushed in the hand to break the pot wall and allow the roots to grow out more easily. Plants with fine root systems are often unable to penetrate the pot wall and so it is sometimes necessary to peel off the fibre pot.

Plastic planter bags are not used during the propagation process but are frequently used once the propagated plants become large enough for growing on. They are made from black polythene and range in size from PB ¾ to PB 95. The most popular sizes for growing on are PB ¾, PB 2, PB 3, PB 5 and PB 6½.

Rootrainers are an innovation that has revolutionised the growing on of young seedlings to the planting-out stage. Rootrainer is a trade name and the general concept is sometimes referred to as a 'book planter'. They are in units of four and open out flat for easy packing and storage. When folded together the two halves interlock at the top so that each cavity or cell resembles a deep narrow pot. The units pack vertically into special wire baskets that hold them together and facilitate carrying. The Rootrainers are then filled with a potting mix and the young seedlings pricked out into them. Larger seeds can be sown directly into them. They can also be used for rooting cuttings of more easily rooted plants. Rootrainers are available in two sizes.

Mist propagation systems

These are designed to spray a fine mist over the cuttings and rooting medium to reduce moisture loss from the cuttings and to create a cool humid environment. It is usually necessary to use some form of bottom heat to offset the effects of lower temperatures. Electronic controls ensure that the mist is provided intermittently and only when needed. Misting systems are used mainly indoors, but they can be used outdoors in areas sheltered from strong winds.

A more recent development of the misting system is that of 'fogging'. The two systems are similar, but a fogging nozzle breaks up the water into extremely fine droplets that remain suspended in the air for much longer periods than the mist droplets. A fogging system keeps a very thin film of water over all surfaces of the cuttings and maintains a very high humidity. It also uses less water.

Bottom heating

In addition to electrical heating cables and the small heating pads available for proprietary propagation cases, there are larger heating pads made especially for horticultural use. They are very easy to use as it is only a matter of plugging them in to a power supply. Heating cable units suitable for home propagators are available from commercial sources. These are simply laid backwards and forwards over the bottom of the propagation bed with no more than 15 cm between each run of cable.

Knives

Traditionally, the budding knife was regarded as an essential item for every plant propagator. Nowadays many propagators use disposable-blade knives instead. Such knives are commonly used for making softwood and semi-hardwood cuttings. Budding knives have a folding blade and are mainly used for budding, bench grafting and making cuttings. Good-quality budding knives are expensive and nowadays the range and availability is very limited.

Secateurs

Secateurs are used for gathering cutting material and for making hardwood cuttings. Two kinds are available: bypass secateurs, in which the main cutting blade slides past the other with a scissors-like action; and anvil secateurs, in which the blade cuts down onto a narrow metal strip or anvil. Bypass secateurs are the most commonly available. Like all cutting tools, secateurs must be kept sharp and the pivot pin should be regularly oiled. When closed, the blades of a pair of bypass secateurs should not have any perceptible gap between them. If there is, it usually means they have been forced or wrenched by cutting stems that are too large. Once this has happened it is almost impossible to make them good again.

Scissors

Scissors can be used for making a range of cuttings, particularly softwood and semi-hardwood cuttings of plants that have thin, easily cut stems. They are also useful for removing leaves from cuttings where removal by hand is too tedious or leaf removal tears off some of the bark. It pays to have one pair of scissors used exclusively for making cuttings. The pivot pin needs to be frequently oiled and the blades should be kept well sharpened. Most scissors have their cutting edges ground to a fairly low angle, but for making cuttings the blades should be ground off so that the angle of the cutting edge is more acute. When fully closed only the tips of the blades should be touching. If held up to the light, it should be possible to see a very narrow gap between most of the length of the blades. Medium-sized scissors 13–18 cm long are most suitable for making cuttings.

Floats

Floats are used for levelling and firming the propagation medium when preparing containers for sowing seed or for inserting cuttings. Usually they are an oblong piece of wood about 2 cm thick with a handle on the back. If seeds are sown in pots and other small containers, it is necessary to have one or two round floats and a small oblong one.

Dibbers

A dibber is used for making holes when transplanting young seedlings. An alternative name is 'dibble'. They are usually pieces of dowelling about 15 cm long with a bluntly pointed end. Two or three sizes are necessary for handling different-sized seedlings, for example from 5 mm in diameter up to 20 mm.

Very small seedlings are difficult to pick up with the fingers and so a special tool made from a wooden spatula or other suitable material is necessary. It should be no more than 2–3 mm thick, about 1 cm wide x 10–12 cm long, and have one end narrowed to 3–4 mm with a V-shaped notch cut into it. The seedling is supported in the notch while being pricked out.

Chopping blocks
Chopping blocks are sometimes used when making cuttings of plants that have thin, rather hard stems, particularly those with very short internodes such as *Leptospermum*, some hebes and *Gaultheria*. A small chopping block can be made from a piece of 2 cm-thick timber. The upper surface is rounded so it is slightly convex, making it easier to use. Scissors have superseded the use of chopping blocks but home gardeners could still find them useful.

Sharpening stones and strops
These are essential for maintaining a sharp edge on knives with permanent blades. A leather strop is necessary for the final finishing of the sharpening process. For making a leather strop a piece of good-quality leather about 2–2.5 mm thick should be obtained. It should be large enough to cut into two pieces about 25–30 cm long x 5–6 cm wide. A piece of timber 1–1.5 cm thick is cut to the same width as the leather and about 10 cm longer so that a handle can be formed. The pieces of leather are then stuck to each side of the board with a suitable adhesive. After the knife has been sharpened on the stone it is finished off on the strop. One side of the strop should have some fine emery paste rubbed into it and that side is used first.

Other equipment
When propagating plants, labelling and record keeping are just as important as the actual propagation. Label containers with the date, the correct name of the plant and any other pertinent information. Plastic labels are the best for this as they are quite long-lasting and easily obtainable. Special quality marker pens with reasonably permanent ink are available. For short-term use, an ordinary lead pencil is quite suitable.

In addition, a notebook should always be kept handy when sowing seed or making cuttings. Good records of dates, methods and results are important and will help to build up a good knowledge of the propagation requirements of various plants.

For grafting, some kind of tape is necessary for

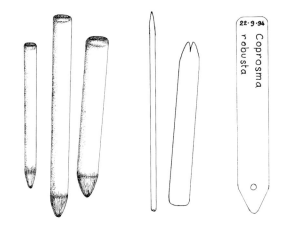

Left: different-sized dibbers.
Centre: a very thin dibber and special tool used for handling minute or delicate seedlings during pricking out; the seedling is carried in the notch of the tool.
Right: the recommended way to write a label.

tying the grafts. Special grafting tape can be purchased, but a very acceptable substitute is plumber's thread tape.

PROPAGATION MEDIA
The provision of a good propagation medium is most important for all plant propagation methods.

For the best results a good medium needs to have the following qualities:

- It must not expand or shrink excessively when wet or dry.
- It should be able to retain moisture for reasonably long periods but at the same time be sufficiently free-draining that it does not hold excess moisture.
- The medium must remain well aerated.
- It should be free of weed seeds, and harmful pests and diseases.
- The pH should be optimum for root initiation (5.5–6.5) or the growth of seedlings.
- It should be able to support cuttings firmly in place.
- It should provide suitable conditions for the germination of seeds and the growing on of seedlings.

A number of different materials can be used for propagation media, either alone or as mixtures. Many plant propagators have their own preferences. The following are the main materials.

Peat
This is one of the most commonly used materials. It is sterile, light in weight, has relatively good water-holding properties and is generally well aerated. One

13

of the main disadvantages of peat is that when it dries out it can be extremely difficult to re-wet it. It is also readily available, although overseas environmental pressure is mounting against the use of peat because of the destructive effects its extraction has on the environment.

Peat occurs in two main forms: moss peat and sedge peat. Deep layers of moss peat formed underneath ancient sphagnum bogs from the long-dead and partially decomposed remains of sphagnum moss. Young moss peat is lighter in colour and provides better aeration. Moss peat has a pH ranging from 3.2 to 4.5. Sedge peats are derived from sedges, sedge-like plants, rushes and grasses that grew in shallow water. Their dead remains accumulated underwater to gradually build up layers of peat. Sedge peats are darker and more decomposed than moss peats, often weedy, and are either acidic or alkaline, with pH of 4.0–7.5.

Moss peat can be purchased pre-packed in small lots suitable for home garden use or, if close to the source of supply, it can be obtained by the truck load. Some of the pre-packed moss peat sold in New Zealand has been pulverised and is really too fine to give good results, in contrast to the moss peat sold in the northern hemisphere.

Bark

In horticulture bark is being used in increasing quantities, either alone or in mixtures with other materials. In New Zealand it is exclusively pine bark, which is a readily renewable resource obtained as a waste product. Already many nurseries use it as a substitute for peat, thus easing the pressure on threatened bog lands.

Bark is available in a number of different grades, but it is the finer grades of crushed bark that are mainly used in propagation activities. Fresh bark should be left outdoors in a moist heap for at least 6 weeks before use, which allows time for toxic substances to dissipate and helps to increase its water-holding capacity.

Finely crushed bark for use in seed-sowing mixes should have a particle size of 6 mm or less. For rooting cuttings better results are obtained if the bark is mixed with peat and/or other materials because bark alone is prone to rapid drying out. For container mixes a slightly coarser grade of bark is generally used.

More recently a prepared grade of bark, known as neutralised bark, has become available. It is graded to produce a good range of smaller particle sizes so that it does not dry out too quickly but still remains well drained. It has had nitrogen, dolomite lime and ground lime added and its pH value is about 6.3. The only preparation it needs is the addition of a slow-release fertiliser.

Sawdust

This is another by-product of the timber industry and some information on bark applies equally to sawdust. Fresh sawdust should be left to age in an outdoor heap for 6–8 weeks as it contains toxic substances. Sawdust that has been composted for a long period is unsuitable because it can break down quickly and become rather soil-like. Coarse sawdust is quite useful in propagation mixes, particularly those used for cuttings. It has good moisture-retention and aeration qualities. Many writers needlessly state that care should be taken to obtain only untreated sawdust. Sawmills always saw timber before it is treated, hence they produce only untreated sawdust. The only establishments that produce treated sawdust are those using treated timber for manufacturing and, in any case, the sawdust is then likely to be too fine.

Sand and grit

Sand is not used commercially as much as it used to be, many growers now favouring bark alone as a medium. Sand is usually mixed with peat, sawdust and perhaps fine bark to create suitable mixtures. It can be used alone for rooting cuttings but tends to produce long, rather brittle roots. Coarse sand gives much better results. The particle size should be 2–5 mm with only a small percentage of fines present. Sand at the coarser end of the scale is generally better and washed sand is preferable. Beach sand should never be used because it is too fine and contains salts which can be harmful.

Grit is finely crushed metal with a particle size of about 3–8 mm. Frequently it is only available when it is produced for spreading on icy roads. In order to remove the very fine particles that cause the grit to compact, it should be washed before use. Grit alone can be used for rooting cuttings but the results are similar to those produced by sand. However, mixed with peat and sawdust, it encourages very good root systems.

Perlite

This is a natural substance used as a soil conditioner. It is a siliceous material of volcanic origin and occurs mainly in New Zealand and the United States. After mining it is heated to about 760°C, which produces a light sponge-like material of a greyish white colour. It is sterile and has good aerating properties. It is best used in mixtures as it will increase their water-holding capacity and provide greater stability for cuttings. When handling dry perlite a dust mask should be worn over the nose and mouth.

Pumice

Pumice is also of volcanic origin and large quantities of it occur in the North Island. It is very porous and so provides good aeration and drainage and is also sterile. It can be used alone but is far better when used in mixtures with peat.

Vermiculite

This is a type of mica that has been expanded by heating so that the particles become soft and spongy. It is very light and able to absorb quite large quantities of water but is now used much less often than previously. If used to excess in mixtures, the mixture is likely to retain too much moisture. When wet it should not be compacted because it does not re-expand.

Soil

Soil is used when propagating seeds and hardwood cuttings in the open ground. It is very variable in quality and unless it has good drainage without becoming too dry, it will need some improvement. Depending upon the nature of the soil, the addition of coarse sand or grit may be required to improve drainage, or humic material such as peat to improve its water-holding capacity.

Some of the foregoing materials can be used alone, but others need to be used in mixtures. Cost, availability and personal preference will determine which media are used for seed sowing, pricking out and rooting cuttings, however all must conform to the criteria listed at the beginning of this section (see p.13). Any mix that does not contain fertiliser can safely be stored for several weeks, although as a general rule only make up sufficient mix for your immediate requirements. After about 6 weeks, mixes containing fertiliser can develop a toxicity that is harmful to plants; if there is any doubt they should not be used.

The following are guidelines only and readers should do their own experiments to find out which mix suits their requirements.

Seed-sowing mixes

Peat, sand and sawdust or finely granulated bark in equal parts make a suitable mix. Alternatively, equal parts of peat, perlite and bark, or 2 parts of peat and 1 part of pumice can be tried. The proportions of any one or more of these ingredients may need to be varied according to their quality. Such mixtures are deficient in nutrients and for the critical post-germination period it is essential that adequate phosphate and calcium are present in the mix. These nutrients can be provided by adding superphosphate (116 g) and dolomite lime (58 g) to 100 litres of mix. A box measuring 60 cm x 60 cm x 28 cm holds 100 litres and can be used for measuring the ingredients.

Some growers include a fungicide but this may damage some tender seedlings so is best avoided if you are uncertain of the possible effects. Good hygiene and correct management of the propagating facilities will go a long way towards obviating the necessity to use fungicides.

When only limited quantities are needed, small bags of a proprietary mix are available from garden centres.

Pricking-out mixes

A mix similar to that for seed sowing can be used but it must contain more nutrients in order to provide for the greater demands of the growing seedlings. To 100 litres of mix add a 6-month slow-release fertiliser (35 g) and dolomite lime (30 g).

If the seedlings are to remain in the mixture for any length of time regular feeding with liquid fertilisers may be necessary. A commercial potting mix should also be suitable providing it is used only for vigorous seedlings, as it could contain too much fertiliser for small and slower-growing seedlings.

Potting mix

A potting mix is similar to a pricking-out mix but contains more fertiliser, usually a larger quantity of a long-term slow-release fertiliser.

Some proprietary potting mixes are mainly peat with only token amounts of bark and pumice added. They are little better than using straight peat as they have a tendency to remain soggy, to the detriment of some plants, and care has to be exercised with watering.

Rooting mixes

Media for rooting cuttings are quite varied and everyone has their own preferences. A good rooting mix must be able to provide sufficient moisture for the cutting, be well aerated and be able to hold the cuttings firmly in place until they have produced roots. The type of rooting mix may affect the quality of the root system produced. For example, when rooted in sand, cuttings may produce long, coarse and brittle roots, whereas when rooted in a mixture of peat, sand and sawdust or any similar combination, the roots are well branched, more compact and not as coarse. Not all species respond to the one rooting mix and sometimes a little experimentation is necessary. Various combinations of peat, sand, sawdust or bark, perlite and pumice should be tried. A good starting point is to try the various combinations using equal parts of each ingredient and then altering the ratios in the light of the experience gained. In addition, the following variations could be tried:

3 parts peat: 1 part perlite or pumice
2 parts peat: 1 part perlite or pumice
3 parts peat: 1 part sand or grit

2
Propagation from Seed

Native conifers and flowering plants produce a wide variety of different seed types. The seeds not only vary enormously in size but also in their form and methods of distribution. They range from the tiny spore-like seeds of the orchids to those of the karaka, tawa and taraire, which are among the largest. Most native daisies have light bristly seeds that are dispersed by wind. The biddy biddy (*Acaena* spp.) is well known to sheep farmers and all who frequent mountain and hill country. Each seed has a barbed spine that immediately attaches itself to anything suitable that may brush against it. The seeds of many native plants are embedded in succulent or dry fruits that are eaten and distributed by birds. The parapara (*Pisonia brunoniana*) produces large clusters of very sticky fruits that become attached to the feathers of any bird large enough to pull them free of the cluster. These are just a few examples of the diversity of native plant seeds.

Although most nurseries propagate the majority of their plants by vegetative means, propagation by seed is still the most widely used method throughout horticulture, agriculture and forestry.

Seed offers a cheap and efficient method of propagating large quantities of plants, particularly where genetic variation is unimportant or can be controlled. Compared to vegetative propagation, simpler and less expensive facilities are usually required. For revegetation projects it is usually quicker and easier to propagate from seed. Seedlings are generally faster growing than plants raised by other means.

There are also disadvantages to seed propagation. The genetic variation may be so great that it is not possible to produce a fairly even line of plants. Seasonal variations sometimes result in particular batches of seeds being difficult to germinate or having very low viability. If a species is dioecious, it is impossible to identify the sex of a particular plant until it flowers. Seed of a particular species may not always be available. Native beeches (*Nothofagus* spp.) often have only one good seed year every 5–7 years. During the intervening years it may be difficult to obtain adequate quantities of seed. With some species seed can take up to 3–5 years to germinate.

To successfully raise plants from seeds the following conditions must apply:

- The seed must be viable and capable of germinating.
- Sufficient moisture must be present in the seed-sowing mix to allow germination to occur.
- The mix should remain well aerated and allow an adequate supply of oxygen to reach the seed.
- The seed must be germinated within its preferred temperature range. For most plants a range of 15–21°C is suitable, with 15–18°C being the optimum. For many hardy plants satisfactory germination may occur at 10°C. In general, a suitable temperature for germination is at least 5°C above the minimum temperature required by the plant when growing.
- Seeds of most plants require light for germination. For a small group of plants light may inhibit germination, however light sensitivity mainly affects freshly harvested seed and tends to disappear after a period of dry storage. Seed germinated in darkness must be moved to lighter conditions as soon as the seedlings emerge. Seeds of some species require full light for germination but little is known about native seeds in this respect.

The sowing times for different species vary widely. Early spring probably suits many species, but it will depend on the growing facilities available and your local climate. If suitable facilities are available it may be possible to sow at other times such as autumn. Further information concerning the treatment of different genera can be found in chapter 7.

SEED DORMANCY

Even if all of the foregoing conditions are provided, there is still no guarantee germination will occur. This is because many seeds have what is known as a dormancy factor.

This is a complex subject and little is known about dormancy in native plant seeds. Seeds of some species have little or no dormancy and others have a limited dormancy that usually disappears after a short period of dry storage.

The seeds of many other native plants fail to

germinate quickly when placed in what appear to be ideal conditions for germination. This is presumably because of internal mechanisms that control the commencement of germination. It is nature's way of protecting the seeds from germinating at the wrong time of the year when they may not survive. There are several kinds of seed dormancy and each requires different treatments to overcome them.

Some growers do not worry about treating seeds to overcome seed dormancy. They claim that mixed results are obtained from species to species and from year to year and that there is little difference between treated and untreated seed.

Physical dormancy (seeds with hard coats)
The hard seed coats prevent water uptake until natural processes have sufficiently softened the seed coat to allow the entry of moisture. The longer such seeds remain in dry conditions the harder the seed coat becomes. Native genera exhibiting this type of dormancy include *Carmichaelia, Notospartium, Sophora* and *Clianthus*. The seeds of some of these plants can remain viable for very many years and seeds of *Carmichaelia 'juncea'* have been germinated after being stored on a herbarium sheet for 140 years. Several treatments can be used to overcome physical dormancy.

HOT WATER: Place the seeds in a heat-resistant container, pour hot water over them and cover well to prevent the water from cooling too quickly. The water temperature should be 77–90°C. For species with slightly softer seed coats, such as *Clianthus puniceus*, the temperature should be 50–77°C.

Leave the seeds to soak for 12–24 hours and for up to 48 hours if the seed is old. At the end of this period remove the water, mix the seeds with a small quantity of moist seed-sowing mix and leave for a further 24 hours before sowing.

SCARIFICATION: This involves cracking, puncturing or reducing the thickness of the seed coat. There are various ways of doing this. The seed coat can be abraded with a triangular file or piece of sandpaper fixed to a block of wood, or it can be chipped with a suitable hand tool. These methods are quite tedious, especially if the seeds are small and difficult to hold. Some authors recommend lining a screw-top jar with a piece of sandpaper. The seeds are put in the jar, which is then vigorously shaken. It takes quite a long time to abrade the seed coats and not many people will have the patience to do this. Whatever method is used, the seeds should be sown immediately after scarification.

HARVESTING IMMATURE FRUITS: The seeds of some species are often capable of germinating even though the fruit enclosing the seeds is not quite mature. Immediately sowing seed from immature fruits can give improved germination as the seed coats have not had time to properly harden.

Mechanical dormancy (woody seeds)
The seeds of some plants are enclosed inside a woody or stony endocarp or outer covering, which may allow water to enter but be too strong to allow the embryo to expand during germination. Softening of the endocarp usually results from microbial activity in the soil. Two main treatments are used to overcome this kind of dormancy.

HOT WATER: Treatment is the same as for physical dormancy.

WARM-MOIST STRATIFICATION: The seeds are stored under warm moist conditions, usually at a temperature of 21–24°C for 1–12 weeks, depending on the species.

Soak the seeds in water for 24 hours. Seeds with a fleshy covering should be cleaned first. Drain off the water, mix the seeds with 3–4 times their own volume of a moist medium such as sand, peat or sawdust, place in a polythene bag and seal it. Thin-walled bags are preferable to thicker ones. Place the bag in a warm site where the required temperature range can be maintained—inside a hot-water cupboard but not on top of the cylinder is often ideal. Regularly check the contents in case they become too dry and moisten if necessary. Sow immediately at the end of the required storage period.

Physiological dormancy
There are various other forms of dormancy caused mainly by biochemical processes, either within the seed or seed coat, or sometimes by a combination of

Ake ake (Dodonaea viscosa) *fruits*

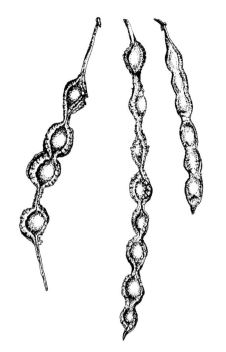

Seed pods of kowhai (Sophora *species*).
Left to right: S. microphylla, S.tetraptera, S. prostrata.

both. Dormancy may also be caused by rudimentary or undeveloped embryos.

The seeds of some plants have incompletely developed embryos and require a period of 'after-ripening' before they are able to germinate. In general, such seeds benefit from a period of warm-moist stratification, or alternating periods of warm-moist stratification and cold-moist stratification, depending on the species. Species in the Ranunculaceae, Araliaceae, Apiaceae, Ericaceae and Gentianaceae may have this kind of seed dormancy.

The freshly harvested seeds of many herbaceous plants have a physiological dormancy that may disappear after a period of dry storage. They may require warm temperatures for germination and, according to the species, may fail to germinate if the temperature is below 10–15°C. Others, such as seeds of the grasses, are light sensitive and may not germinate if the seeds are covered.

COOL-MOIST STRATIFICATION: Soak the seeds in water overnight, or for 24 hours if they have hard seed coats. Clean any seeds that are enclosed in fleshy fruits. Then drain off the water, mix the seeds with 3–4 times their own volume of a moist medium, put the mixture into a polythene bag and seal it. Leave it at room temperature for 3–4 days to enable the seeds to take up as much moisture as possible, otherwise the chilling period is less effective. Place the bag in a refrigerator set at about 3°C. Gently shake the bag once a week to keep the seeds well aerated and

moisten the mix as required. Most species require only 4–12 weeks refrigeration, after which they are sown immediately.

OUTDOOR CHILLING: The chilling requirements can also be met by placing the sown seed outdoors over winter, although this is less effective in mild areas.

In autumn sow the seed in a container and cover with a layer of grit or coarse sand, which will help to prevent the growth of liverworts and algae over winter. Put the container in a cold shady place such as on the southern side of a building or fence and leave it there over winter. Protect emerging seedlings from slugs and snails. In spring the container can be moved to a cold frame or greenhouse to encourage germination.

SOWING SEEDS IN CONTAINERS

REQUIREMENTS: Clean containers, seed-sowing mix, seeds, fine dry sand, small screed board, 5–6 mm sieve, watering can, atomising spray, floats, labels, pencil or marker pen, and a sheet of glass or polythene film.

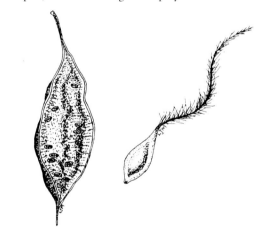

Left: kaka beak (Clianthus puniceus) *seed pod.*
Right: the 'seed' or achene of Clematis; *the plumed tail or style enables the seed to be carried by wind.*

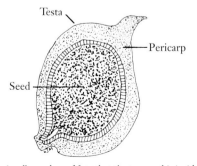

Ranunculus *'seed' or achene. Note that the true seed is inside a dried carpel. Numerous carpels make up the seed head of the* Ranunculus.

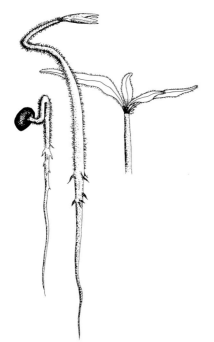

Stages in the growth of a germinating kohuhu (Pittosporum tenuifolium) *seedling. Each seed leaf (cotyledon) is divided into two and gives the impression that there are four instead of two.*

PROCEDURE:

1. Use only clean containers. If the container is dirty, wash it clean and then soak for about 15 minutes in a solution of 1 part of household bleach to 20 parts of water.

2. If necessary, water the mix so that it is evenly moist but not too wet. Loosely fill the container with the mix and remove the surplus. Using a float, lightly firm the mixture so that its surface is level and about 1–1.5 cm below the rim of the container. Firming the mixture too much will reduce aeration and drainage and hinder seedling growth. Remove any large lumps from the surface. For fine seeds it may be necessary to sift a little mix over the surface.

3. Sow the seeds. Avoid sowing them too thickly as overcrowded seedlings quickly become drawn and spindly and are more prone to disease. Sow systematically from side to side across the container and sow as evenly as possible.

4. Sift a little mix over the seeds to cover them. The general rule is that the depth of the cover should be 1–3 times the diameter of the seeds. Small seeds should not be covered to any more than their own diameter and larger seeds should be sown at the greater depth. The growth of liverworts and algae over the surface of the mix can be troublesome, so when seeds are likely to take several months to germinate, cover them with grit or coarse sand rather than seed-sowing mix.

5. Label the container and water lightly with a fine-rose watering can. During bright weather shade the container with a sheet of newspaper.

Fine seeds

To sow very small seeds evenly they are best mixed with fine dry sand, using 3–4 times the quantity of seed. The container should be watered before sowing to avoid washing away the seed. After sowing, damp down the seed with an atomising spray bottle.

Very fine seeds do not need covering with mix, but keep the surface of the mix moist. Slightly larger seeds may benefit from a very light covering, although seeds of *Leptospermum* and *Kunzea* usually germinate quite well if left uncovered. Seeds of grasses such as *Chionochloa* and *Poa* are probably better left uncovered because they are sensitive to being covered too deeply.

Some fine seeds germinate better if the container is covered with a piece of clear glass because it helps to maintain the humidity around the seeds. The glass should be turned at least once a day to allow the condensation forming on its undersurface to evaporate, otherwise there is the risk of damping off or some other fungal disease. The glass will not be required for some species if germinated in an enclosed space such as a cold frame or greenhouse and provided a suitable atmosphere is maintained. Newspaper shading is unnecessary unless the container is in direct sunlight.

Medium seeds

Sow such seeds much more thinly than smaller seeds and gently firm them into the mix with a float. Always wipe the bottom of the float clean of any seeds that may have stuck to it. Where practicable, seeds can be individually sown into containers such as cell trays, eliminating the necessity for pricking out and resulting in quicker growth of the seedlings.

Large seeds

Depending upon their size, large seeds can be either scattered or placed singly. The largest seeds, such as those of karaka, tawa and taraire, are probably better sown singly at regular spacings in the container. Generally, these seeds are simply pressed in to the mix to about half their diameter, but they can be gently firmed into the surface with a float and covered to a depth equalling their own diameter. Alternatively, they can be sown in containers such as cell trays.

Sowing seeds in outdoor beds

Preparation of the seed bed should commence some months before sowing. Dig over the soil and work it into a reasonably fine tilth. Sand or grit may be required to improve drainage or humic material added to make it more friable. Cultivate the surface frequently to eliminate any weeds present and to encourage any dormant weed seeds to germinate.

REQUIREMENTS: Seed, labels, pencil or marker pen, rake, hoe, sieve and shading materials or shade covers.

PROCEDURE:

1. Just prior to sowing, cultivate the upper 10 cm of soil to bring the surface to a fine tilth and rake it level.

2. Either broadcast the seeds or sow them in drills. After broadcasting, gently firm the seeds into the surface and cover to a depth 2–3 times their own diameter. Take out drills of the correct depth with a hoe, the back of a rake or a pointed stick, sow the seeds and fill in the drill. Water as necessary.

In general, seeds in outdoor seed beds should be covered to a slightly greater depth than those sown in containers, because of the erosive effects of wind and rain, and the more rapid and prolonged drying of the soil surface. Exceptions requiring little covering such as the daisy family are discussed under 'special sowing techniques' on page 21. Covering the seeds with coarse sand or grit will help retain moisture, reduce compacting or crusting, and weeds are easily removed.

Seedlings are often left in outdoor seed beds until autumn, when they are either lined out in the open ground or potted, so avoid sowing the seeds thickly.

3. Place the shading materials or covers into position. If manuka brush is used, the pieces are pushed into the ground along either side of the seed bed so that their tops meet above the bed. Covers should be supported at least 40–50 cm above the seed bed.

AFTERCARE

It is critical that the seed-raising mix or soil does not dry out during germination, and so the containers or seed bed should be checked regularly. Often all that is required is a spray with an atomising spray bottle as a watering can may make the mix too wet, but it is also necessary to check that the mix is not drying out deeper down. Good ventilation is also important and as much as possible the optimum temperature should be maintained. A temperature that is too high can inhibit germination as much as one that is too low. Shading the containers from bright sunlight until after the seeds have germinated is also crucial.

The appearance of mould on the medium surface indicates inadequate ventilation or excessive temperatures. A watering or spray with a fungicide such as Captan will generally control it providing the conditions causing the problem are rectified.

Emerging seedlings can be very susceptible to damping off. The best means of control is to maintain the correct environment, avoid over-watering and maintain good hygiene. Adopt the measures outlined above for the control of mould if it appears.

The germination of many native plant seeds can

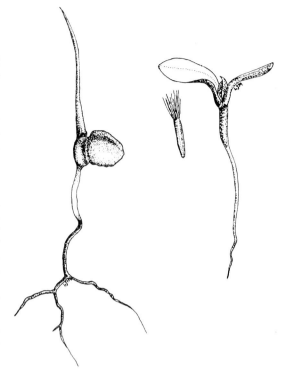

Left: a typical monocotyledon seedling (Cordyline) *showing the single seed leaf emerging.*
Right: a typical dicotyledon seedling (Celmisia) *showing the two seed leaves (cotyledons); a seed is also shown.*

be very erratic and can vary from year to year. If germination has not occurred within what you feel is a reasonable time, do not hastily discard the container and contents. *Cyathodes* seed, for instance, can take up to 3 years to germinate.

The period from germination until pricking out is also a critical stage. Any inattention at this stage can be detrimental to the seedlings. From spring until autumn some shading is usually essential. If the seedlings are being grown in a greenhouse or cold frame, shade cloth is probably the best means of providing shade. For seedlings grown outdoors, shade covers or brush wood can be used. Small quantities being grown in a plastic bag or small propagation case should be kept in a well-lit situation but not in direct sunlight. To avoid fungal diseases such as damping off ensure there is good ventilation and don't allow conditions to become cold and damp or excessively hot and damp. Protection from slugs and snails is particularly critical.

PRICKING OUT

Pricking out is the transplanting of small seedlings

into pots or trays where there is more space for them to grow. The object is to obtain sturdy young plants that can be planted directly into the open ground or further grown on in pots or planter bags. In general, seedlings should be pricked out as soon as possible after germination, but there are always exceptions. If they are left too long, the transplanting shock is often greater.

Slower-growing seedlings are often better left until they have produced 2–3 true leaves. The seedlings of some plants appear to be gregarious and make far better growth when in fairly close proximity to each other. In my experience the pohutukawa (*Metrosideros excelsa*) is an example of this. For such seedlings it often pays to prick them out once at quite close spacings, and again at wider spacings when they have made sufficient growth.

Very small seedlings do not like being put into a deep mass of pricking-out mix that is slow to dry out and remains wet and cold for long periods. For the first pricking out the mix should be only about 3 cm deep and for the second pricking out should be at least 5 cm deep. After pricking out, keep the seedlings in a greenhouse, cold frame or other protected conditions for at least a few days to recover from the transplanting shock.

Special sowing techniques

Although the great majority of seeds can be grown by the methods already described, some require different techniques to facilitate germination. These techniques are mainly used for plants with very small seeds and which may require special habitat conditions for germination. Some alpine genera, such as *Donatia*, *Gaultheria* and *Dracophyllum*, are typical examples, as are most orchid species. Fern spores also require a special technique.

Anyone familiar with nature will have noticed how some seeds and spores germinate with the utmost freedom on moist clay road banks, whereas others germinate very freely in clumps of moss or moss-like plants. It is possible to simulate such conditions so that these plants are more easily raised from seed or spores.

Scree technique

This technique imitates the conditions provided by a clay bank and the depleted but stable ground bordering many shingle scree areas. It is mainly suitable for small seeds that do not always germinate readily when sown in the conventional manner. *Celmisia*, *Myosotis*, *Gentiana* and *Raoulia* are some of the genera that benefit from this technique. Many species sown according to this technique often germinate within 3 weeks to 1 month.

REQUIREMENTS: Seed, suitable containers, sowing mix, floats, 10 mm stone chips or coarse grit, labels, pencil or marker pen, and watering can.

PROCEDURE:
1. Spread a single layer of 10 mm stone chips or coarse grit over the surface of the mix. With the stone chips it should be just possible to see the mix between some of the chips. The grit particles, being smaller, provide a slightly denser cover.
2. Scatter the seeds over the gritty surface layer. The fluffy seeds of the daisy family do not always easily fall between the stone chips so it is often preferable to sow the seeds before applying the stone chips or grit.
3. Label the container and lightly water with a fine-rose watering can.

Bog technique

This technique imitates the conditions provided by moss cushions, the low hummocky plants that grow in many bogs, and the conditions that occur in pakihi areas. In all instances seeds frequently land among plants that are saturated or nearly saturated so that there is a continual supply of moisture, but at the same time they have the aeration essential for germination. There are two ways of providing these conditions.

REQUIREMENTS: Seed, seed-sowing mix, sphagnum moss, clean containers, small screed board, floats, sieve, labels, pencil or marker pen, watering can, atomising spray bottle, and a sheet of glass or polythene film.

FIRST METHOD:
1. Fill the container with seed-sowing mix and water it.
2. Rub some sphagnum moss through a sieve with a mesh size of about 1 cm and spread a layer 5-8 mm thick over the surface of the mix. Before sieving, moisten the sphagnum to prevent it from breaking up too finely. If the moss is too fine algae will soon grow on it and may inhibit germination. Sow the seeds on the moss and moisten with an atomising sprayer.
3. The container should be kept under close conditions in a propagation case or covered with a piece of glass or polythene if placed in a greenhouse. Only water with an atomising sprayer; the mix under the moss should not be allowed to dry out. Once the seedlings are well up they should be gradually hardened off before being pricked out.

SECOND METHOD:
For this method it is preferable to use a shallow container no more than about 5 cm deep. A small punnet is ideal. If a deeper container is used fill it to a depth of only about 4 cm.
1. Fill the container with seed-sowing mix and sow the seeds. The seeds will not need to be covered. Make

sure that the mix is very free-draining.
2. Place the container in a tray or dish that is as deep as itself. Fill the tray or dish with water to half the depth of the mix and maintain the water at this level.
3. Once the seedlings have produced their first true leaves, progressively reduce the water level over 3–4 days before removing the container from the water. Harden off the seedlings before pricking out.

Growing orchids from seed
Orchid seeds are usually sown under sterile conditions in flasks containing a specially prepared medium of agar jelly and essential nutrients. However, there is a simpler technique that can be used by home gardeners.

To raise some of our native terrestrial orchids from seed it is first necessary to have plants growing in containers. Ripe seed of the appropriate species is scattered over the surface of the potting mix around the base of the plant, which is watered as usual. All being well, small orchid seedlings should appear during the following growing season or possibly even later.

For those wanting to grow our epiphytic species (*Dendrobium*, *Earina*, *Drymoanthus* and *Bulbophyllum*) from seed the following method can be tried. It is an old technique and is detailed by Elliot and Jones in the *Encyclopaedia of Australian Plants* (vol. 1, 1980). I have not tried it myself.

REQUIREMENTS: A new clay flower pot 12–15 cm in diameter, sphagnum moss (moisten before rubbing through a 10–15 mm sieve), finely chopped tree fern

fibre, peat and a piece of new towelling 25 cm x 25 cm or 30 cm x 30 cm, according to the size of the pot being used.

PROCEDURE:
1. Sterilise the clay flower pot by boiling in water for 15 minutes.
2. At the same time prepare a mixture of equal parts of sphagnum moss, fern fibre and peat and lightly moisten it.
3. Fill the pot to about one-third full with the mixture and firm it into place.
4. Take enough of the remaining mixture to almost fill the rest of the pot and put it on the piece of towelling. Gather the corners of the towelling tightly together so that the mixture is formed into a ball and tie with a piece of string.
5. Push the towel-encased ball firmly into the pot, ensuring that the tied corners are underneath. There should be a 2–3 cm space between the top of the towelling and the rim of the pot. Some sphagnum moss packed between the outside of the towelling ball and the wall of the pot will help to reduce evaporation.
6. Sterilise the whole by pouring boiling water over it and wait for it to cool.
7. Sprinkle the orchid seed over the surface of the towelling. In order to provide the all-important mycorrhizae, a few tips of live orchid roots should be scattered among the seeds. Without them germination may not be successful.
8. Cover the pot with a sheet of glass and stand it in a deep saucer containing boiled water. Place in a greenhouse or some other protected environment and keep shaded. Maintain the water at a depth of about 3 cm.
9. Germination should occur within a few weeks and is indicated by the presence of fine fungal threads around the seeds. The seedlings should be ready for pricking out after about 12 months or possibly up to 2 years.

Growing ferns from spores
Ferns are the only plants dealt with in this book that are propagated by spores. The spores are produced without the aid of two sexes and are incapable of directly producing a new fern plant. Under suitable conditions the spore grows into a prothallus, which is a small green scale-like structure that is usually somewhat heart-shaped. The prothallus bears the male and female reproductive organs. Moisture is required to enable fertilisation to occur and it is only then a new fern plant can develop.

Growing ferns from spores is a most fascinating means of producing new ferns. It is not too difficult and only requires a little patience and attention to hygiene. Some ferns are more difficult to raise from spores than others and if you have never tried it

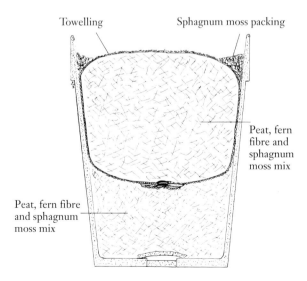

Towelling   Sphagnum moss packing

Peat, fern fibre and sphagnum moss mix

Peat, fern fibre and sphagnum moss mix

How to prepare a pot for sowing orchid seed

before, it is better to commence with some of the hardier and easier species.

REQUIREMENTS: Fern spores, small punnets or 10-12 cm diameter pots, seed-sowing mix, sieve, bucket, boiling water, labels, marker pen or pencil and clear polythene bags large enough to take individual containers.

PROCEDURE:
1. Loosely fill the container with moist seed-sowing mix and, using a float, lightly firm the mix so that the surface is about 15–20 mm below the rim of the container. The surface layer should be fine and without any large lumps. If necessary, sift some fine material over the surface.
2. Place the container in the bucket and pour in boiling water until it is up to the rim of the container. When pouring the boiling water take care not to disturb the surface of the mix. Leave it to soak for about 5 minutes before removing and allow to drain and cool. This is to kill any unwanted spores of liverworts, mosses and other ferns.
3. Sow the spores and moisten with an atomising spray bottle. Spores may be sown from a broad knife blade. Pick up some spores on the tip of the blade and gently tap the blade to scatter the spores. Alternatively, a piece of paper, folded in half so that it becomes V-shaped, can be used.
4. After labelling place the container in a polythene bag and seal with a twist tie. It is preferable to germinate the spores in a low-light situation and, depending on the species, the temperature should be 15–24°C. Bottom heat could also be helpful during the cooler months. Check the container regularly to ensure the mix is continually moist. If necessary, use an atomising spray bottle to remoisten it.
5. Germination of the spores is indicated by the appearance of a bright green, fine, moss-like growth on the surface of the mix. At this stage the temperature should be a little cooler at about 14–20°C. If kept too

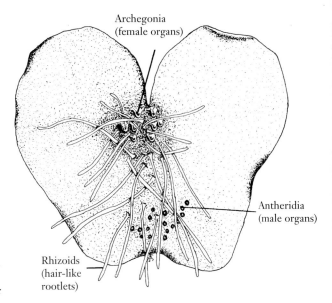

Archegonia (female organs)

Antheridia (male organs)

Rhizoids (hair-like rootlets)

Detail of the underside of a fern prothallus

warm the development of the prothalli could be retarded. According to the species, the prothalli may be slow to increase in size and some can take up to a year to mature.
6. Once the prothallus has matured and fertilisation has occurred, the true fern will then develop. Fast-growing species can produce the first true fronds within about 8 months from sowing. Slower-growing species can take 12–18 months before they produce true fronds. At first they are often pricked out in small clumps and are later separated when they are large enough. To avoid transplanting shock, place them in a polythene bag for about 10–14 days and keep shaded from direct sunlight. The bag can then be opened for longer periods each day until the young plants are sufficiently hardened off.

3
Propagation from Cuttings

Growing plants from cuttings is the most common method of asexual propagation — that is, using pieces of vegetative plant material instead of seed (sexual propagation).

One of the main advantages of vegetative propagation is that all of the progeny are identical to the parent plant, which is important when a high degree of uniformity is required. It avoids problems such as seed dormancy, poor viability and the difficulty of obtaining seeds of certain species. Vegetatively propagated plants may flower at a much earlier age than those grown from seeds. It enables the propagation of superior forms of particular plants and is the main method of propagating clones that will not reproduce true to type from seed or cannot be propagated from seed.

Disadvantages of vegetative propagation are: it is more expensive than growing plants from seed; better facilities are required; and diseases such as viruses are more readily transferred from plant to plant.

To successfully grow plants from cuttings the following must apply:

- The plant must be capable of producing adventitious roots from some part of the stem or, in the case of root cuttings, to produce a new shoot system as well as a new root system.
- Suitable healthy material must be chosen from the parent plant and must be taken at the most suitable time of the year. The parent plant should not be stressed for any reason such as lack of water when the cutting material is taken.
- The material must be kept cool and turgid from the time of collection until the cuttings have been inserted in the rooting mix.
- Use a rooting mix that will hold the cuttings firmly in place, be well aerated and provide sufficient moisture.
- The cuttings must have sufficient water and humidity, adequate light without being exposed to excessive or direct sunlight, and the rooting mix should be kept at the correct temperature.

TYPES OF CUTTINGS

Cuttings are classified according to the part of the plant from which they are obtained. Stem and root cuttings are the two main types used in the propagation of native plants, but leaf cuttings are very occasionally used. Stem cuttings include softwood, semi-hardwood, hardwood, nodal and internodal, and heel cuttings.

Softwood cuttings

These are made from soft succulent shoots and are usually taken in spring and early summer, although softwood cuttings may be obtained from some plants at other times of the year. Generally, they should be taken early enough in the season to allow the resulting plant to produce some mature wood before winter sets in.

Although softwood cuttings often root more easily and quickly than other types of cuttings, they also require more care and attention. Typically, the cuttings will be about 7.5–10 cm long, although for some plants they may be shorter.

Material should only be gathered from stock plants with firm turgid growth and which are not under stress from dry conditions. Shorter side shoots should be chosen in preference to rapidly growing and very sappy leading growths, which are likely to collapse. A good test as to the suitability of the material is to bend the shoot at a right angle; if it snaps, the material is suitable, however there are exceptions to this rule.

After collection the cutting material should be kept cool and moist to prevent wilting. The cuttings should be prepared and inserted into the propagation medium as soon as possible. Softwood cuttings can be made with a knife or a pair of sharp scissors. Some form of bottom heat is desirable, although it is possible to root softwood cuttings in unheated propagation facilities as long as conditions are generally warm. For many species rooting often occurs within 2–4 weeks.

For some species the time of the year when softwood cuttings can be rooted is quite specific and may be as short as 2–3 weeks. In this respect little is known about native plants and it is only through experimentation that our knowledge will be improved. From early November until early December would be the most likely period for such experimentation, although other times of the year should also be considered.

Some authorities also distinguish 'herbaceous cuttings'. These are softwood cuttings taken from herbaceous plants and to all intents and purposes are little different from other softwood cuttings. For New Zealand native plants, the term would mainly apply to some alpine plants.

Semi-hardwood cuttings

Semi-hardwood cuttings are made from stems that are intermediate between the softwood and woody stages. The latter occurs when the growth ripens and becomes mature. They are the most widely used type of cutting and a very wide range of plants can be propagated by this means.

Depending on their degree of firmness, semi-hardwood cuttings can be subdivided into:

- Soft semi-hardwood: the shoots are still growing but their lower portions have taken on a degree of firmness and they are becoming woody.
- Firm semi-hardwood: much of the shoot is becoming woody.

Semi-hardwood cuttings are generally 7.5–15 cm in length, but with some species (e.g. *Leptospermum* cultivars) they can be up to 20 cm. With quite small shrubs, such as some *Hebe* species, they may be as short as 25 mm. As a general rule, short side shoots are always preferable to strong-growing leaders, which may look good but are usually unsuitable. Most semi-hardwood cuttings can be made with a knife or pair of scissors. Although semi-hardwood cuttings do not wilt as readily as softwood cuttings, they should still be kept cool and moist immediately after gathering. Leaves and side shoots are removed from the lower half of the cutting and, if it is a large-leaved plant, the leaves are reduced in size.

The traditional time for taking semi-hardwood cuttings is from about February until April or May but for many plants they can be taken year-round. Many native trees and shrubs have several flushes of growth throughout the year and so it is usually not difficult to find suitable material. For some species August to October is less suitable because the cuttings may try to make top growth instead of producing roots and so may be quite slow to root.

Hardwood cuttings

These are made from mature wood that has become quite hard. Overseas the main plants propagated from hardwood cuttings are deciduous trees and shrubs and coniferous plants, but quite a wide range of native plants can be propagated by this method. Hardwood cuttings are usually taken during late autumn or early winter when the plants are more or less dormant. There are two kinds of hardwood cuttings — those that are rooted indoors and are usually 12.5–18 cm

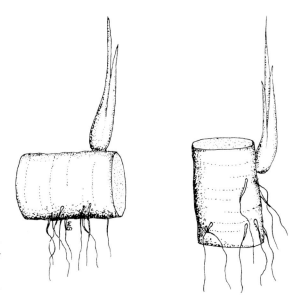

Stem section cuttings of Cordyline banksii *(left) laid horizontally and (right) inserted vertically*

long, and those that are rooted in the open ground and are 20–25 cm long. The latter method is not much used nowadays but is still a very easy technique.

Short hardwood cuttings are made in the same manner as semi-hardwood cuttings. Long hardwood cuttings are selected from more vigorous growths because it is often difficult to obtain lateral growths that are long enough. The basal leaves and side shoots are removed, leaving about one-third to one-quarter of the foliage. Any soft sappy tip growth should also be cut off as it will only wilt. The base of the cutting is usually trimmed just below a node with a knife or pair of secateurs.

A variation that can be used for propagating two *Cordyline* species is a 'stem section'. It can only be used for *C. banksii* and *C. pumilio*, which have relatively thin stems. A piece of the stem is cut into sections 3–4 cm long. The sections can be laid horizontally and pushed into the rooting mix until they are half buried or they can be set vertically into the mix. Bottom heat is necessary to encourage rooting.

Nodal and internodal cuttings

A node is the joint on the stem where a leaf is attached or a bud arises. Nodal cuttings are sections of stem with the basal end trimmed just below a node. With some plants, such as some *Hebe* species and members of the Epacridaceae and Ericaceae, the nodal joints are very close together and it does not matter where the basal cut is made because it will always be close to a node.

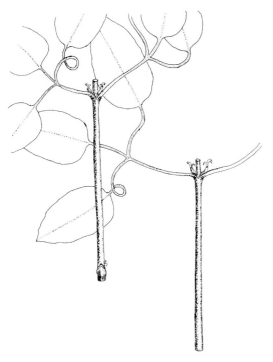

Nodal (left) and internodal (right) cuttings of Clematis.

Root cuttings

For some plants pieces of root cut into short lengths and inserted in a rooting mix are capable of producing new shoot and root systems. Little is known about the ability of native plants to regenerate from root cuttings but present knowledge indicates only a very small number can do this. *Drosera binata* is one which can be grown from root cuttings. *Linum monogynum* and kohekohe (*Dysoxylum spectabile*) are also reputed to grow from root cuttings. Experimentation is necessary to discover whether root cuttings are successful for any other native plants.

Root cuttings are usually taken in late winter or early spring as growth is about to commence. Unless a plant has quite large roots, root cuttings are usually about 25–50 mm long and to encourage growth they should be kept in a greenhouse or under similar conditions.

The prepared cuttings can be treated in two ways. They can be laid horizontally on the surface of the rooting mix and covered with mix as for seed sowing. Alternatively, insert them vertically into the mix with

Internodes are the portion of the stem between two nodes. Internodal cuttings have only one node at the top of the cutting. The basal end of the cutting is trimmed immediately above the lower node. The native *Clematis* and *Rubus* species are examples of plants that can be propagated from internodal cuttings, but as they grow just as easily from nodal cuttings there is little reason for using them. Internodal cuttings are an advantage when cutting material is limited because a greater number of cuttings can be made.

Heel cuttings

A heel cutting is a shoot torn from the parent stem with a small portion or 'heel' of the old wood attached to its base. Normally the rough surface of the heel is trimmed with a knife, but in some instances better results may be obtained if only the ragged bits at the bottom end of the heel are trimmed. Heel cuttings may be taken for both semi-hardwood and hardwood cuttings. The cuttings of some species have been found to root more readily if they have a heel, but it is a matter of experimentation to determine which method gives the best results. Heel cuttings can be particularly useful when cuttings are being grown in a cold frame and may take a long time to produce roots. They are also quite useful when propagating some native conifers from cuttings.

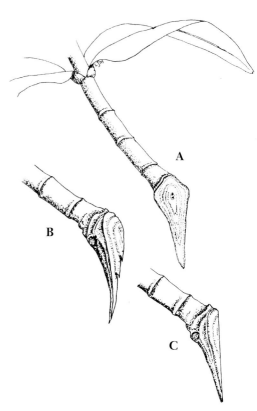

Heel cutting.
A: the cutting after it has been torn off the parent plant.
B: profile of the untrimmed heel.
C: profile of the heel after it has been trimmed with a knife.

the tops of the cuttings just below the surface. However, you must maintain the correct polarity, so cut the end nearest the plant square across and trim the basal end with a diagonal cut.

A variation of the root cutting is the 'toe' produced by *Cordyline* species and cultivars. The toe is part of the root system and is a thick fleshy extension of the stem, like a kind of taproot, that grows deeply into the ground. On young plants the toe may be up to 6–8 cm long and if carefully removed can be treated as a root cutting. Its removal does no harm to the parent plant. The toes should be inserted vertically into the rooting mix.

Leaf cuttings

This is not an important propagation technique for native plants. However, one native genus that can be propagated this way is *Drosera*. In this instance the leaf blade and petiole are used for starting new plants. Roots and a shoot form adventitiously at the base of the petiole and develop into a new plant. The original leaf eventually withers away.

COLLECTING AND HANDLING CUTTINGS

Age of the parent plant

This is one of the most important factors relating to the selection of material for cuttings. Cuttings taken from young plants generally produce roots more quickly and easily than those taken from old plants. Sometimes there is no choice over the source of material. The only plant available may be many years old and the only thing to do is to select the most suitable material. When there is a choice between a young plant and an older one, cuttings should be taken from the young plant every time.

Time of year for taking cuttings

As already explained there are optimum times of the year for taking some types of cuttings or cuttings of certain species, but for some plants cuttings may be taken at almost any time providing suitable material is available. For example, if long hardwood cuttings of *Brachyglottis*, *Olearia* and *Hebe* species are to be successfully rooted outdoors, they need to be taken during early winter. Alternatively, if being rooted indoors it is possible to take short hardwood cuttings of these plants from about February until May.

Some species have quite specific periods when cuttings can be taken and successfully rooted. For some it may be a period of no more than 4 weeks or so and if cuttings are taken at any other time the success rate is likely to be minimal. Very little is known about which native plants have such specific requirements.

Type of material

The first rule is that only good quality material should be collected for cuttings. The stock plant should be in good health and as far as practicable the material should be free of any obvious pests and diseases. If propagating from plants that have been grown from seed, be careful to take material from a plant with good qualities, particularly with regard to growth and form, and which is obviously superior to the others.

In general, only non-flowering shoots should be taken for cuttings, as flowering shoots may be putting too much energy into flower production and may not be in such good condition for producing roots. This is not always possible because some plants, such as certain hebes, flower over a very long period. With such plants all that can be done is to remove all flowers when the cuttings are made. In any case, *Hebe* cuttings usually root quite easily so that the presence of flowers is not so critical.

Except when taking material for long hardwood cuttings, short side branchlets or lateral shoots of the desired length are the most suitable. Sometimes it is possible to take slightly larger branchlets on which there will be a number of lateral shoots that are all suitable for cuttings. With other species it may be possible to take longer shoots from which several cuttings can be made.

Occasionally there are plants on which the growth is short and gnarled and virtually no suitable cutting material is apparent. A search inside the bush may reveal a few lateral growths that could be more suitable.

When selecting material for long hardwood cuttings it is necessary to take longer and somewhat more vigorous shoots than would be chosen for short hardwood cuttings.

Another important factor is the position on the plant from which the cuttings are taken. With the great majority of plants it is not a problem, but can be with coniferous plants in particular. If cuttings are taken from lateral branches there is a strong possibility that the resultant plants will have a spreading growth habit and a reluctance to produce leading shoots. Thus cuttings should be taken from more vertical branches which exhibit what is known as 'apical dominance'. It applies particularly to native conifers such as the podocarps *Libocedrus* and *Agathis*.

Care of cutting material

When gathering material for cuttings you will need a pair of secateurs, some polythene bags, labels and a pen or pencil. If the cuttings are to be made straight away it will be sufficient to just moisten the inside of the polythene bags, but if it is going to be some time before the material is handled, wrapping it in damp newspaper will keep it in good condition. As each batch of material is collected it should be labelled and put into a separate bag to avoid any possible confusion.

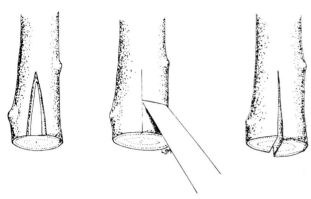

Different ways of wounding the bases of cuttings.
Left: slice wound; a slice is taken off the outside of the stem.
Centre: incision wound; the point of the knife is used to make
one or more slits down the base of the cutting.
Right: split wound; the basal end of the cutting is split, the cut
usually being made with a pair of secateurs.

Some books lay considerable stress on the necessity to gather cutting material in the early morning or late evening, since temperatures are cooler and the material will be in the best possible condition. This is not always practicable and, providing cutting material is properly cared for, the collection time is not critical.

If you will be away for several days, there is nothing worse than arriving home to find that the cutting material has become overheated in the car and is useless. A small insulated cooling bin will enable the cuttings to be kept cool and moist until they are brought home, or they can be stored in sealed polythene bags in a refrigerator for several days without causing them any great harm so long as the cuttings do not freeze. However, the cuttings should be made as soon as practicable after collection to ensure greater success.

AIDS AND TECHNIQUES FOR ROOTING CUTTINGS

Various aids and techniques can be used to assist the rooting of cuttings and to improve the strike rate.

Wounding

Wounding can be useful for semi-hardwood and hardwood cuttings that are difficult to root, especially if they have older wood at their bases. For some species it may make the difference between failure and success. Cuttings of coniferous plants often require wounding to induce rooting but for the majority of species wounding is unnecessary. It may also sometimes induce basal rotting or allow the entry of harmful pathogens.

The simplest form of wounding occurs when the lower branchlets or leaves are hand stripped from the cutting. With some species quite large amounts of bark are removed at the same time, in which case the branchlets or leaves should be removed with a knife or pair of scissors. If a knife is used, the cutting should be held upside down and the branchlets or leaves removed from the base of the cutting towards the tip.

A slice wound involves slicing a shallow sliver 2–3 cm long off the basal end of the cutting. For short cuttings the length of the wound may need to be reduced to about 1 cm. The depth of the slice will depend on the diameter of the cutting and the thickness of the bark. Shallow wounding is generally preferable to heavy wounding and only sufficient bark should be removed to expose a reasonable amount of the inner tissue.

For plants that do not readily root around the stem, a double-slice wound can be tried. This involves removing a second slice of tissue from the opposite side of the stem.

Another method is to use the point of a knife to make a series of vertical cuts 2–3 cm long at the basal end of the cutting. Usually, the cuts are evenly spaced in series of two, three or four. Each cut must be deep enough to penetrate the bark and into the wood. The length of the cuts will depend on the length of the cutting and may need to be shortened to about 1 cm.

A method practised for many years by home gardeners is to split the base of the stem to a depth of about 1 cm. It is known as incision wounding and can be particularly effective on hardwood cuttings. A pair of secateurs or knife is used. The split was sometimes held open by placing a grain of wheat in it. Apparently there is some scientific support for this. Once the cutting has been planted the wheat grain germinates and in so doing produces auxin, which is also required for root initiation.

Leaf reduction

When making cuttings of large-leaved plants it is necessary to reduce not only the number of leaves per cutting but also the size of the remaining leaves. This reduces the amount of water transpired by the cutting, makes the cuttings easier to handle and enables them to be inserted closer together. Large overlapping leaves may also encourage disease, block out valuable light and prevent the rooting mix from being properly moistened.

The aim should be to remove one-third to half of the original leaf area. After the lower leaves have been stripped from the cutting, the remaining leaves are trimmed with a pair of scissors or a knife.

Removal of terminal growth buds and flower buds

The importance of removing flower buds from

cuttings has already been mentioned, but with cuttings of some species it may also be advantageous to remove the terminal bud or shoot tip. This is the case with some South African species of *Erica*. Removing the soft growing tip helps to prevent vegetative growth, thus giving the cutting a better chance of producing roots.

Little is known as to whether any native plants are similarly responsive, but some experimentation with members of the Epacridaceae (e.g. *Cyathodes*, *Epacris*, *Dracophyllum*) could prove to be worthwhile.

Rooting hormones

These are synthetic growth regulators used to hasten root initiation on cuttings and to increase the strike rate. They also increase the number, quality and uniformity of roots. However, they are not a substitute for good propagation practices. They may not be necessary for cuttings that root easily, but for those that are more difficult they can be a definite advantage.

The two chemicals mainly used are indolebutyric acid (IBA) and naphthaleneacetic acid (NAA), with IBA probably being the most widely used. They are commonly available in powder form but gel and liquid forms are also available.

The concentration of the active ingredient varies, for example from 0.1 to 0.8%. The lowest concentration is recommended for softwood cuttings and the highest for hardwood cuttings. However, different species respond in different ways to the various concentrations and the best advice is to experiment to find which gives the best results for a particular species.

The powder hormones are very easy to use as it is simply a matter of dipping the moistened ends of the cuttings into the powder. Never dip the cuttings into the original container; tip a small quantity into another container, as moisture and bits off the cuttings will cause the hormone to deteriorate and become useless. After use any surplus powder should be thrown out. The gel is used in a similar manner except that it is unnecessary to moisten the ends of the cuttings.

Liquid hormones are diluted to the desired strength and can be used in two ways: soaking and the quick-dip method. Soaking uses a more dilute solution and cuttings are stood for 24 hours in 2.5 cm of the solution. The quick-dip method requires a stronger solution and the base of the cutting is dipped into it for no more than 3–5 seconds.

To prevent deterioration occurring, store the containers in a cool dark place when not in use. A refrigerator is ideal. Warm temperatures and light cause the active ingredient to gradually break down so that it soon becomes useless.

AFTERCARE

Inserting the cuttings

During the process of inserting the cuttings in the rooting mix they should be graded according to size so that all cuttings of more or less equal length are together. That prevents smaller cuttings from being overshadowed by larger ones and means they all receive equal light and it also helps to prevent disease.

Long hardwood cuttings are usually rooted in the open ground and normally they would be set out during June. In districts that experience cold winters it is good practice to callus them in boxes of damp sawdust before lining them out during late August or early September. For pre-callusing, the cuttings should be put in a cool place with good air circulation and adequate light. Avoid direct sunlight and water the sawdust if at all necessary.

For rooting long hardwood cuttings outdoors it is necessary to have a cutting bed, which is prepared as for an outdoor seed bed (see chapter 2). It should be sited where it has some protection from wind and does not receive full sun for the whole day. An ideal situation is where it receives some shade during the middle of the day.

Ensure the bed is kept free of weeds and watered whenever necessary. As well as keeping weeds down, mulching between the rows helps conserve soil moisture and keeps the soil surface cool during hot weather. The cuttings are left in the cutting bed until late autumn or early winter when they can be lifted. Those that are large enough can be planted in their permanent positions. It is usually preferable to line the remainder out in the open ground to grow them on for another season.

Rooting temperatures

The temperature of the rooting medium greatly influences the rooting of cuttings. Easily rooted cuttings will strike well at ambient temperatures, which will usually average 12–15°C. Some species may root within 7–10 days. Even some difficult species will root in cool conditions, but they may be slow to do so, especially over winter.

Cool conditions are most useful from spring until autumn, but bottom heat greatly increases the range of species that can be rooted and often the ease of rooting. With bottom heat, the optimum temperature for the rooting medium should be 18–21°C, although some species will root at a slightly higher temperature (up to 25°C).

The air temperature around the cuttings should not be any warmer than necessary. High air temperatures can be injurious to cuttings, causing defoliation and sometimes death. They also tend to stimulate vegetative growth at the expense of root development and increase water loss from the leaves.

From spring until autumn, daytime air temperatures of 21–27°C are quite satisfactory. During winter, temperatures of 12–15°C are sufficient, although warmer temperatures are an advantage.

Maintenance and hygiene

These are two of the most important aspects of cutting propagation. Both need regular attention if problems are to be avoided.

Most home gardeners will not have misting or fogging systems and so it will be necessary to check frequently and manually maintain a humid atmosphere around the cuttings. An atomising spray bottle can be used to spray water over them and during very warm weather it may be necessary more than once a day. Water the rooting mix whenever necessary. With bottom heat the mix tends to dry out from the bottom up and so the mix should be regularly checked accordingly. Shading with a sheet of newspaper or shade cloth may be necessary during hot weather.

There should be a daily check for fungal diseases, which can be quite devastating if allowed to go unchecked. A number of diseases can affect cuttings during propagation and strict attention to hygiene is essential. Some fungal diseases such as *Phytophthora* and *Pythium* are soil borne, but *Rhizoctonia* can be carried on the cuttings themselves. Grey mould (*Botrytis cinerea*) may suddenly appear, usually as the result of poor ventilation and warm humid conditions.

The propagation facilities should be kept clean and tidy at all times, and old plant material should not be left lying around in the vicinity. Remove dead leaves and any dead or infected cuttings. It is also good practice to carefully remove the rooting mix immediately around a diseased cutting and replace it with new mix. As a precaution, spray the cuttings with a fungicide such as Captan.

Some propagators routinely dip all newly made cuttings in a fungicide before inserting them into the rooting mix, but others spray with a fungicide during the time they are in the propagation case or cutting bed. However, good hygiene and cultural practices will go a long way towards preventing the necessity for spraying.

4
Grafting, Layering and Division

GRAFTING

Grafting is the act of joining a part of one plant onto another in such a manner that their tissues will unite and they will continue to grow as one plant. It is one of the oldest known methods of plant propagation and is very useful for plants that would otherwise be difficult, although for native plants it has limited application. The technique is not difficult and with practice is easily learned.

Grafting requires a rootstock or understock plant and some scion wood. The rootstock is the plant onto which the graft is made and becomes the root system for the new plant. Rootstocks are usually raised from seed or sometimes from cuttings. The scion is a short piece of stem taken from the plant to be propagated.

It is essential that the rootstock and the scion are compatible and capable of uniting to form a permanent union. In general they must be closely related for grafting to be successful. For example, variegated cultivars of karaka (*Corynocarpus laevigatus*) can be grafted onto seedling rootstocks of the ordinary green form, but it is impossible to graft variegated broadleaf (*Griselinia littoralis* 'Variegata') onto a karaka because they belong to different families.

For a successful graft union it is critical that the cambium layers of the rootstock and scion are in close contact. The cambium cells divide to produce what is known as callus tissue between the rootstock and the scion. This healing of the graft union is an important part of the grafting process.

A number of different methods of grafting exist but the main techniques used for propagating native plants are side grafting and top-wedge grafting. These are usually carried out during late winter and early spring. It is important that grafting is done before the scion wood has burst into growth. If necessary, the scion wood can be collected up to 1 week beforehand and stored in polythene bags in a refrigerator.

For the grafting operation a suitable knife, such as a budding knife, a sharpening stone and some grafting tape are required. Plumbers' jointing tape is a good substitute for grafting tape.

Side grafting

With this method the scion wood is grafted onto the side of the stock, which is left intact until the graft has taken. There are two main variations: the side-veneer graft and the side-wedge graft. Both are commonly used for propagating evergreen plants.

For side grafting it is necessary to prepare the rootstocks well ahead. Seedlings about 18 months to 2 years old are usually suitable for rootstocks and they should already be established in containers. A stem diameter of 5–10 mm is ideal for most plants. About 2–3 weeks before grafting, the rootstocks should be put in warmer conditions so that their growth is slightly more advanced than that of the scion. That encourages the graft union to heal more quickly.

Side grafting may also be used for producing plants grown as standards. Some *Hebe* species and cultivars, for example, can be grafted onto tall rootstocks to produce standards. In this instance a vigorous species such as *H. barkeri* is used to produce the tall rootstock to the desired height. A scion of a suitable species or cultivar is then side grafted onto the upper part of the rootstock.

Side-veneer graft

PROCEDURE:

1. Ensure the lower 6–8 cm of the stem of the rootstock is free of leaves and branchlets.
2. On the smoothest part of the clear stem make a shallow downward and inward cut 2–3 cm long. Make a second, slightly downward cut just above the end of the first, so that a chip of wood is removed leaving a small step at the bottom of the cut. The depth of the step should be approximately one-third of the diameter of the stem.
3. The scion should be from the current season's growth, 10–15 cm long, as thick as or slightly thinner than the rootstock, with a prominent terminal bud that has not yet burst into growth. Remove the leaves from the basal 3–5 cm and cut the base of the scion to match the cut on the rootstock.
4. Insert the scion in place, matching the cambium layers as closely as possible. If the scion is thinner, ensure that it matches with one side of the rootstock.

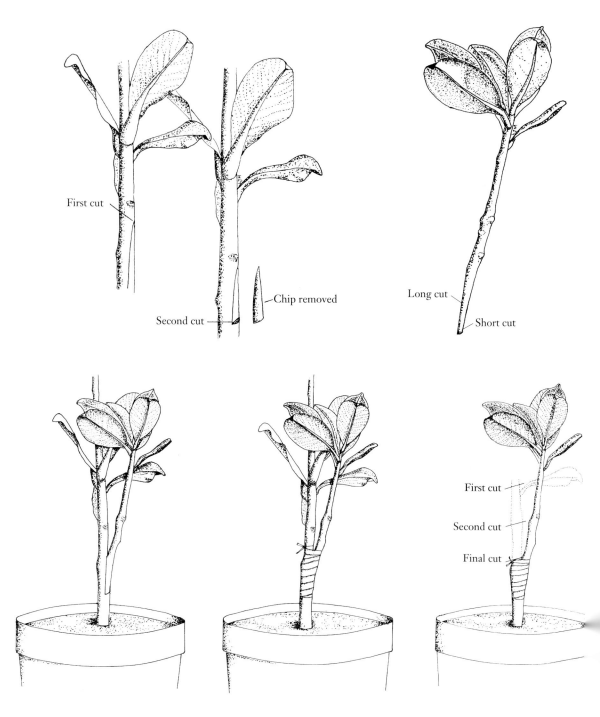

First cut

Chip removed

Second cut

Long cut

Short cut

First cut

Second cut

Final cut

The various steps in making a side-veneer graft.
Top left: a long shallow cut is made into the rootstock, followed by a short, slightly downwards cut at the base of the first; the small chip of bark and wood is removed.
Top right: the scion is prepared by making a long, sloping cut on one side and a second short cut on the opposite side of its base; these cuts should match those made on the rootstock.

Above left: the scion is inserted into the rootstock so that the cambium layers match on at least one side.
Above centre: it is then tied tightly with grafting tape and placed in warm humid conditions.
Above right: when the graft has taken the top of the rootstock is cut back in stages; this is normally done over a period of 8–12 weeks

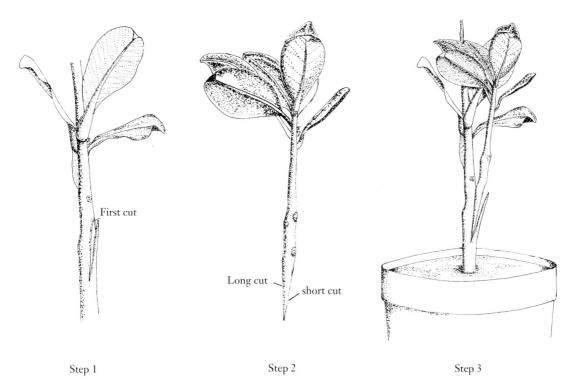

First cut

Long cut — short cut

Step 1   Step 2   Step 3

The various steps in making a side-wedge graft.
Left: a long and shallow, sloping cut is made into the rootstock.
Centre: the scion is prepared by making a long, sloping cut on
one side and a shorter cut on the other.
Right: the scion is inserted into the rootstock with the longer cut
innermost; it is then tightly tied with grafting tape.

The graft is then tightly wrapped with grafting tape. Make sure that a space is left between each turn.

5. Place the grafted plant in a warm humid environment such as a propagation case or polythene tent. Bottom heat maintained at 18–20°C is ideal, but a steady air temperature of 15–18°C will probably suffice. The containers should be stood on a moist base such as sand, rooting mix, peat or sawdust to help maintain a constant humidity. Without bottom heat a little more care is required. In trying to maintain the correct humidity ensure that the grafts are not kept too cold and wet.

6. After the union has healed, the stock above the union is cut back gradually. The appearance of callus growth between the turns of the tape indicates that the graft has taken.

Side-wedge graft

This is very similar to a side-veneer graft and for the beginner, it is easier than a side-veneer graft. On the smoothest part of the base of the rootstock make a shallow downward and inward cut 2–3 cm long,

leaving a thin flap of stem attached by its base. The base of the scion is cut to a wedge shape so that it will neatly fit into the cut on the rootstock. Both cuts should be straight and even. Some propagators prefer to make the wedge unequal so that the cut on one side is longer than the other. When the scion is inserted into the cut on the rootstock the longer side goes against the stock and the shorter side against the flap. Because the scion has two cuts, callus is able to form on both sides. Apart from the different cuts, the steps for making this graft are the same as for the side-veneer graft.

Top-wedge graft

As with the two previous methods, the rootstock should already be growing in a pot. With a sharp pair of secateurs, cut off the top of the rootstock about 3–4 cm above soil level. Using a sharp knife, make a vertical split 2–3 cm long in the top of the rootstock. Cut the scion to length (about 10–12 cm) and, using a knife, trim its base to a wedge shape about 2–3 cm long. If possible the diameter of the scion should equal that of the rootstock. Insert the scion into the split on the rootstock, taking care to match the cambium layer on at least one side and tightly wrap the graft.

AFTERCARE: The aftercare for the three methods is identical. Maintaining the correct temperature and humidity is of utmost importance. Shading with

33

A —— B

A and B cuts of equal length

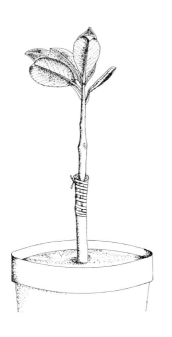

newspaper or shade cloth is necessary in hot weather. At higher temperatures greater attention will need to be paid to maintaining the humidity. The grafts should be regularly ventilated and lightly sprayed with water afterwards. Water the rootstock whenever necessary.

When watering or spraying to increase the humidity, take care not to over-wet the graft union as that can be detrimental. Always handle the grafts with great care because they are fragile and easily damaged for quite some time.

About 3–6 weeks after the grafts have taken, gradually increase the ventilation periods to harden them off. Hardening off should be completed by about 8–12 weeks after grafting. At that stage the covering can be completely removed, but it may need to be replaced by shade cloth. During hardening off the top growth of the rootstock should be reduced by about half. That is normally done about 6–8 weeks after grafting. About 6 weeks later the terminal bud of the scion should have burst into growth and the remaining top growth of the rootstock can then be reduced to 2.5 cm above the graft.

The tying material should be carefully removed once the union has obviously healed and before the stem shows signs of constriction. From then onwards the grafted plant is fully hardened off until it can be grown on outdoors. About 4 months later the remaining stub, on the side grafts, should be neatly cut off just above the graft union. Remove any growth appearing from below the graft union with a sharp knife.

LAYERING

Layering is one of the simplest and easiest ways of propagating plants. It involves encouraging the development of adventitious roots on a stem while it is still attached to the parent plant. Once a viable root system has formed the stem is severed and becomes a new plant in its own right.

Some low-growing plants layer themselves naturally when their creeping stems root as they spread. The stems of larger shrubs may sometimes come in contact with the ground and develop roots, however with quite a number of trees and shrubs layering can be induced artificially. For the home

The various steps in making a top-wedge graft.
Left: the top growth has been cut off the rootstock which has been split to receive the scion.
Centre: the scion is prepared by making two equal cuts on either side.
Right: the scion is inserted into the cleft of the rootstock and tightly tied into position with grafting tape.

gardener it is a very good means of propagation when only 1 or 2 plants are required and is often successful for plants that are difficult to root from cuttings.

There are several different techniques, but the only ones applicable to the propagation of native plants are simple layering and aerial layering.

Simple layering

Simple layering is probably the most widely used technique. It may be carried out almost all year round but the best times are spring and autumn, with spring probably giving the best results.

It requires a branch that can easily be bent down to allow the younger growth to be pegged down below soil level. Root formation may take about 5 months to 2 years or more. The best wood for layering is 1 year old. Older stems can be successfully layered but rooting may be very slow. It is usual to wound or treat the stem to encourage root production.

The soil should be friable and well-drained. If necessary mix in humic material or sand.

The pegs can be made from wire or wood. I prefer wood because it is less likely to pull loose from the soil. Wire pegs should be 20–25 cm long and made from 8- or 12-gauge wire. Wooden pegs are easily made from suitable stems off a tree or shrub. Choose pieces that are straight for about 20 cm and have a side branch diverging at an angle.

REQUIREMENTS: Suitable pegs, knife, trowel, short bamboo canes and tying material.

PROCEDURE:
1. Bend over the stem to be layered so that it touches the ground at a point about 25–30 cm from its tip. Scoop out a hollow about 15 cm deep.
2. Wound or treat the stem to encourage the formation of roots. Any of the illustrated treatments can be used.
3. Peg down the wounded portion in the hollow. A short bamboo cane should be used to support the terminal portion upright.
4. Fill in the hollow to cover the layer and carefully firm the soil around it.

AFTERCARE: Little maintenance or aftercare is required. Keep the area weed free and water during dry periods. A light mulch will assist with moisture retention.

Often the only certain way of determining whether the roots have developed is to carefully dig alongside the layer. Rooted layers should be lifted in autumn. During March or early April sever the rooted layer from the parent plant with a pair of secateurs. The cut is made as close to the ground as possible. The layer is then left for about 4–6 weeks before lifting. The remainder of the connecting stem is then cut off close to the root system.

Simple layering

Layers with strong root systems can be planted out directly, otherwise they should be potted and grown on before being planting out.

Aerial layering

By providing the necessary environment, the formation of roots is induced on aerial parts of the plant. When the root system is sufficiently developed the layer is severed from the parent plant and grown on.

In warmer places aerial layering can be carried out all year round, but in cooler regions spring and summer are the best times.

REQUIREMENTS: Moist sphagnum moss, pieces of clear polythene film measuring 18–20 cm x 25–30 cm, tying material, knife and a roll of electricians' adhesive tape.

PROCEDURE:
1. Use strong healthy stems of the current season's growth. Remove the leaves from a mid-point about 20–30 cm below the shoot tip, leaving about 12–15 cm of clear stem.
2. Wound the stem to provide the necessary constriction. The stem may be girdled, which involves removing a 10–15 mm wide ring of bark from around it. A variation of girdling is to remove the bark in two half circles but with the half circles staggered, one above the other so that no part of one meets the other. Alternatively, a slanting, upward cut, similar to that for ground layering, can be made. With the latter it is necessary to ensure that the two cut surfaces are kept apart by inserting a small chip of wood between them, or by twisting the stem so that they cannot come together. The application of some rooting hormone to the cut surfaces may be beneficial.
3. Take sufficient moist sphagnum moss to make a

fist-sized ball, place it around the wounded section and hold it in position with the tying material. The moss should be moist but not wet.

4. Wrap a piece of polythene film reasonably tightly around the moss and secure with the adhesive tape. Black polythene film should not be used because it may cause the layer to overheat.

Roots may be produced within 2–3 months but may take up to 2 years. With slower-rooting layers it may be necessary to check the moisture content of the moss after a few months, but take care not to overwet the moss.

5. Once roots can be observed through the polythene, the layer can be removed from the parent plant. Carefully unwrap it and, without removing the sphagnum moss, plant in a container. Keep it in a suitable environment such as a shade house or a greenhouse until it is well established. For the first 1–2 weeks the rooted layer may be inclined to wilt so keep it in a close atmosphere during that time.

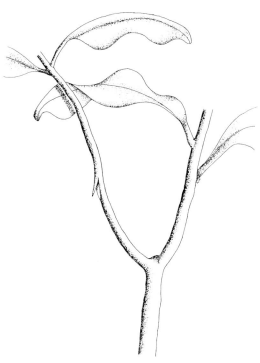

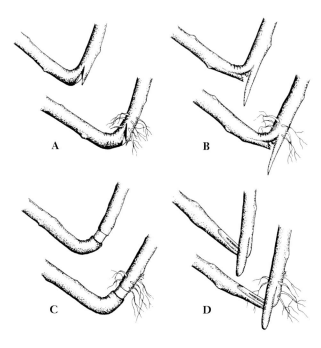

The various ways of wounding stems when layering.
A: a simple cut or incision; the cut should be held open with a small chip of wood.
B: the stem is girdled by removing a narrow band of bark.
C: the stem is cut, on its underside, and then partially broken; the break stays open.
D: the technique is the same as C except that the cut is made on the upper side of the stem; the stem is then twisted as it is bent upwards so that the tongue of wood projects down one side.

The various steps in making an aerial layer.
Left: the stem is wounded either by making an incision or by girdling it; the incision wound should be held open with a small chip of wood.
Centre: a fist-sized ball of moist sphagnum moss is tied around the wounded part of the stem.
Right: the ball of sphagnum moss is then wrapped in clear polythene film, which is sealed with electricians' adhesive tape, note that as well as sealing it top and bottom, the overlapping edges where it wraps around the moss are also sealed.

DIVISION

Dividing plants is one of the simplest and easiest methods of propagation. Generally, it can only be carried out on plants that form clumps, produce rhizomes or have prostrate stems that root as they spread. It is mainly confined to herbaceous plants, but some small shrubs and suffruticose plants that have dense growth with multiple stems arising from below the soil level can also be propagated by division. Some plants are easily divided and can be pulled apart with the hands, but others may require a little more persuasion. Those that form rather dense clumps usually need to be divided with the aid of two garden forks. A spade should never be used unless there is no alternative, as it indiscriminately cuts through roots and shoots and generally does more damage than is necessary. Renga renga (*Arthropodium cirratum*), *Astelia*, *Bulbinella* and

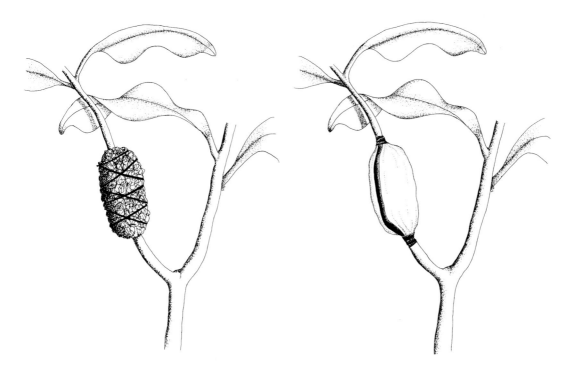

tussock grasses should be divided with two forks.

Division can be undertaken during autumn or spring. Spring is the preferred time especially if the plants are breaking into growth. Division can also be safely done immediately after flowering.

Firstly, dig up the plant to be divided. Push the two forks back to back into the clump and pull their handles apart so that the clump is gradually parted without doing much damage. With large clumps this operation can be repeated several times to produce a number of divisions. Each division should have at least one growth bud or shoot and its own root system. Any long and straggly roots should be shortened by about half to make replanting easier. If the division has large leaves, they should be cut back to half their length to reduce the shock of being divided and transplanted. Divisions should be replanted immediately and watered in well.

Some plants such as *Aciphylla* and *Anisotome* have woody root systems and are not always easily divided by using two forks. It may be necessary to use a sharp knife instead. If the clump is more open, it may be possible to use a pair of secateurs.

Mat-forming plants such as *Raoulia* and *Acaena* are very easily divided by removing rooted pieces from the mat. Unless large quantities are required, pieces removed from the outside of the mat make much better plants than those taken from the centre.

A number of ferns can be propagated by division.

Those with multiple crowns are preferably divided before they grow too large, otherwise the plants receive too much of a setback. Species with creeping rhizomes often divide more easily but some can be difficult. When dividing ferns with multiple crowns ensure that each crown has some root attached and that the parent plant is not damaged in the process. With those that have creeping rhizomes, each portion of the rhizome must have a growing tip.

When a fern plant has been disturbed the fronds very easily wilt and die, so that after division the fronds should be reduced in length or completely cut off, leaving only the stalks or stipites. For ferns that have quite firm or tough fronds it is sufficient to cut them back to leave several of the lower pinnae, but if they have very soft fronds complete removal is preferable.

The divisions should be potted and kept in a humid atmosphere in a shady place until they become established.

SPECIALISED TECHNIQUES

Mechanically induced branching

Some plants, such as *Astelia*, can have a relatively slow rate of branching so that propagation by division may be equally slow. With *Astelia* it is possible to artificially hasten branching by suppressing the apical dominance, which is responsible for the slow rate of branching of the stem.

37

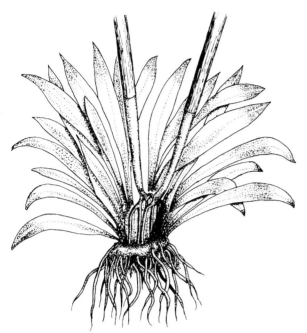

mosses. When detached from the parent they develop into new plants.

In the case of ferns, gemmae are bulbils or small plantlets that develop on the older fronds of certain species. The term 'proliferous' is also used to describe this method of natural reproduction. When large enough they can be planted in some rooting medium and grown on. The only native plant known to produce these plantlets in quantity is the hen and chicken fern (*Asplenium bulbiferum*).

To propagate *A. bulbiferum* by this method, the plantlet should be removed together with a small portion of the frond to which it is attached. That is necessary to enable it to be anchored into the rooting medium.

The portion of the frond is folded downwards, inserted into a hole and the medium firmed into place around it. The bulbous base of the plantlet should be fractionally below the surface. Keep them in a humid

Using two garden forks, back to back, to divide a herbaceous plant

Mechanically induced branching is most easily carried out on a young plant that has not yet produced new growths or off-shoots. If a young *Astelia* plant is sliced in half it will be seen that the tip of the stem forms a basal plate from which the leaves and roots arise.

The object is to remove just the apical shoot so that branching is encouraged from the rest of the basal plate. The first step is to completely cut off all foliage just above the basal plate. Care must be taken not to cut too low down so that the top of the basal plate is sliced off. Cutting off too much limits the number of new shoots that will appear. If the cut is not deep enough to remove the apical shoot it can be carefully scooped out with the tip of a knife blade.

Mechanical induction of branching is best carried out just as growth is about to commence during late winter or early spring, and is better if performed on plants already established in containers.

After about 4–6 weeks the new shoots should appear and the actual division can be undertaken several months later, as soon as the young shoots are large enough to be detached with some root attached.

Gemmae or bulbils

Gemmae are small asexual reproductive structures occurring on some plants, particularly ferns and

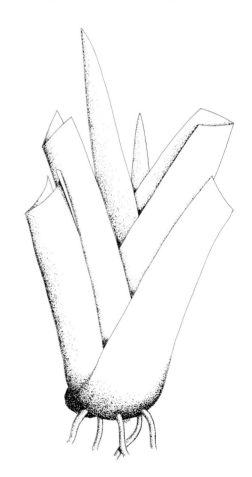

*A 'fan' or single division of flax (*Phormium*) with the leaves cut back ready for planting*

atmosphere until they have produced roots and produce new fronds.

Auricles

Auricle is a name given by some authors to the swollen fleshy jointed base of the stipe of *Marattia salicina* (para or king fern), which is left attached to the rhizome when the frond falls off. The term actually refers to the 2 ear-shaped lobes attached to it and which helped to protect the young frond when it was unfurling. In reality these jointed bases are shaped more like a horse's hoof, which gave rise to one of its earlier common names – 'horseshoe fern'. Auricle is used for want of a better term.

The older auricles can be cut or gently prised off from the lower part of the rootstock. They are then partially buried in some rooting mix with their tops just exposed. The auricles should be kept in a moist frost-free environment until the new plants are produced. It can take 6–12 months for new plants to develop, but the use of bottom heat can speed up their growth. Once one or two new fronds have developed they can then be put into pots for growing on.

5

Harvesting and Storing Seed

When growing plants from seed it is important that only the best-quality seed is obtained and sown. Poor-quality seed and substandard storage conditions will inevitably lead to poor results.

Seed of native plants can be obtained from a number of sources, including wild plants, cultivated plants, exchange schemes and commercial outlets. With the first two the collector can have control over important factors such as whether the seed is from a plant having good qualities, is likely to be true to type, and comes from a geographical area likely to produce plants of the required hardiness. Some plant societies and botanic gardens have seed distribution or exchange lists, which can be an excellent way of obtaining seed of uncommon species, but quantities offered are often small and seed may not always be of the best quality or correctly labelled. A few firms sell seed, but some sell only minimum quantities that would be more than many people require.

The most important points regarding seed harvesting, be it from wild or garden sources, are:

- knowing where different species may be found;
- learning when the seed is likely to be ripe and ready for harvesting;
- choosing a 'mother' plant with superior qualities. Depending on your ultimate aim, it may be better to harvest seed from several trees to obtain a good genetic mix.

FACTORS AFFECTING RIPENING AND HARVESTING

The season when seed becomes ripe and ready for harvesting depends very much on the particular species. The common *Wahlenbergia gracilis* flowers over a considerable part of the year so that ripe seed can be collected at almost any time during the flowering period. Conversely, *W. matthewsii* flowers over a more limited period and so seed harvesting is similarly restricted. The fruit of the native geraniums not only ripens quickly but also has an explosive mechanism for dipersing the seed; therefore, it may be necessary to harvest the seed on an almost daily basis. Many species have more definite periods when their seed can be harvested, but some such as *Pittosporum* and *Sophora* hold their seed for quite long periods and it is often possible to harvest seed for several months after ripening.

Other factors to consider are the various agents responsible for dispersing or eating the seed of different species, for example birds, possums, rats, mice and insects. The soft berries of the wineberry (*Aristotelia serrata*) do not keep well and birds usually eat them quickly, whereas the firmer fruits of *Corokia* keep well and often remain on the bush until late winter. Thus there is not the same urgency when collecting *Corokia* seed as there is with wineberry.

Possums eat the fruit of some native trees and, depending on possum numbers, the seed of some species may be difficult to collect in certain areas. Rats and mice can pose a similar problem. In a year when the beeches (*Nothofagus* spp.) seed copiously, rats and mice may build up to plague proportions and very little seed may be available.

Insects are another problem as their larvae often attack seeds just after ripening. Sometimes their eggs have already been laid on the seed and may not hatch until after harvesting, which means that a large percentage of the seeds could be damaged while in storage. When that is likely to happen, harvest the seed while it is ripe enough to germinate but still slightly green. There is then a good chance that predatory insects have not yet laid their eggs on the seeds. Examples where this occurs are ribbonwood (*Hoheria* spp.) and the pink broom (*Notospartium* spp.). The seed of some daisies such as *Celmisia* spp. are sometimes heavily infested and eaten by caterpillars and it is then difficult to harvest any quantity of viable seed.

Seeds with hard seed coats (e.g. *Sophora* and *Carmichaelia*) are also often harvested when they are slightly green and before the seed coat hardens, but this is to avoid the seed-coat dormancy factor. The ripe seeds of *Ranunculus* barely change colour from green and are quickly shed from the seed head. Accordingly, it is usual to harvest what appear to be unripened seeds. *Clematis* is similar except that the seeds change to a brownish colour.

The seeds of many native grasses and daisies ripen very quickly after flowering and are quickly dispersed by wind.

It is possible to collect spores from some species of ferns over much of the year, but others produce spores for a more limited period. The sori of these species may mature during early spring and are soon dispersed by drying spring winds. It may be necessary to monitor their condition during late August or early September.

Fern spores are easily harvested. Look for fronds that have unopened sori on their undersurfaces, and either cut off the whole frond or, in the case of large ferns, just remove a few of the pinnae. Some ferns produce their spores on special fertile fronds that have a distinctive appearance.

The times of the year when specific seeds are ripe can vary considerably from year to year because of climatic variations and may be advanced or delayed by as much as 6–8 weeks from what is regarded as the norm.

PROVENANCE

When harvesting seed from wild sources one of the most important considerations is the provenance of such seeds—the geographical location and altitude at which the seed was collected. The provenance can affect a number of important factors such as a plant's cold-hardiness and drought-resistance, the viability of the seed, the size, shape and colour of the leaves, resistance or susceptibility to pests and diseases, or overall form and growth habit.

Plant hardiness is particularly important. Seed collected from one locality may be quite unsuited to another. For example, young plants of the commonly grown East Cape form of kohuhu (*Pittosporum tenuifolium*) can be frost-tender in localities subject to severe frosts, whereas seed of this species collected from inland valleys of the South Island or from Southland produce plants that are much hardier to frost when young. This also applies to other species that may extend from lowland areas to higher altitudes.

Unfortunately, many people in the nursery trade do not realise the importance of provenance when obtaining their seed for propagation and all too often produce plants that may be unsuited to particular conditions. A good nursery should keep records of the seed sources of the plants they grow and ideally should grow clones from different areas so that customers can purchase according to their requirements.

The increasing importance being placed on environmental plantings also needs to be recognised. Government agencies, local authorities and private individuals are becoming more involved in such plantings and require plants of the correct provenance; this means obtaining plants that originate from specific geographical areas. Some nurseries already provide this service but more need to be aware of the necessity for it.

HARVESTING SEED

Although it can be tedious, seed or fruit should be hand-picked individually. Cutting off branches to harvest seed is a destructive practice and should be avoided. If large quantities are to be gathered, a bag tied around the waist allows both hands to be used. A short pole with a hook on the end enables branches otherwise out of reach to be pulled closer.

For berrying trees and shrubs an alternative is to lay a sheet of cloth or plastic beneath the tree and lightly beat the branches with a pole.

Gathering fruit off the ground is perfectly acceptable and is sometimes the only practicable way of obtaining seed of taller trees. In season, considerable quantities of seed often litter the ground beneath individual trees.

Genera that produce capsules, such as *Metrosideros* and *Leptospermum*, can retain the unopened capsules for long periods. Manuka capsules sometimes remain on the tree for 2–3 years without opening. They can be collected all year round and the seed will be perfectly viable. The capsules of southern rata (*M. umbellata*) can take 12 months or more to ripen; the pohutukawa (*M. excelsa*) and kanuka (*Kunzea ericoides*) ripen more quickly. Ripening is usually indicated when they change colour from green to brown.

For plants such as *Hebe*, which bear their flowers in compact racemes, it is much more convenient to take the whole raceme when harvesting seed. This is perfectly acceptable as it does no damage to the plant. With grasses and grass-like plants it is also usual to remove the whole inflorescence so that the seed can be threshed out at a more convenient time.

CLEANING SEEDS

After collection the seeds must be cleaned prior to sowing or storage. Cleaning is a time-consuming but important job as it greatly reduces the risk of fungal diseases or other problems.

If they have been harvested into plastic bags they should be emptied into open boxes or, if dry, into open jars and held in a cool well-ventilated place until they can be properly handled. Never leave seeds or fruits in plastic bags for longer than is absolutely necessary.

Seeds in dry capsules or pods can be held until those in fleshy fruits have been cleaned. Some such as renga renga (*Arthropodium cirratum*) are easily removed once the capsules have split open. Rubbing the split capsules between the hands is usually sufficient to free the seeds. Removal of the chaffy remains of the capsules is easily done by winnowing: tip everything into a shallow container 3–4 cm deep and while gently shaking it, blow softly across the top of the seeds. If you blow too hard the seeds will also be blown away. A suitable set of fine-mesh sieves can also be used.

Dehiscing capsules can simply be left in cardboard boxes or paper bags in a warm place for a few days until the capsules split open. The seeds are then easily shaken out and require little or no cleaning. *Hebe*, *Leptospermum*, *Kunzea* and *Weinmannia* are examples of genera that can be treated in this manner.

Pittosporum seeds are among the more difficult to clean. Within the capsule the seeds are immersed in a mucilaginous and very sticky substance. Attempt to remove them by hand and you soon finish up being very frustrated and with seeds stuck all over your hands. Some growers recommend soaking them in a solution of dish-washing detergent, but I have found this to be ineffective. The best way to make them easier to handle is to mix the seeds with some dry sand so they are coated with sand.

The seeds of the native legumes (e.g. *Sophora* and the native brooms) do not readily come free from the pods and it is usually necessary to painstakingly remove them by hand. If a large quantity of kowhai seed is to be cleaned some growers put the pods in a shallow box and, by rubbing a wooden float or similar implement backwards and forwards, crush the pods sufficiently to allow the chaff to be sifted out.

In general, seeds in fleshy fruits should have the flesh cleaned from them. For seeds that are to be stratified or moist stored, the flesh will be removed as part of the process, but for others it should be removed in any case. The easiest way to remove the flesh is to put the fruits in a glass or plastic container, mash or pulp them, then stir in enough warm water to make the pulp liquid. The container is then put in a warm place for 2–3 days to allow partial fermentation to occur. Longer periods of fermentation could cause damage to the embryo inside the seed. A kitchen sieve can be used for washing the pulp from small quantities of seed.

Larger quantities of seed will need to be washed in a deep container such as a plastic bucket. The mixture is poured into the container and a steady (but not vigorous) flow of water is used to float off the pulped flesh and skins. At the same time, the contents are stirred to encourage all unwanted material to flow out with the water. The washed seeds are spread out to dry on some absorbent paper and any remaining skins or other rubbish can be removed by hand.

The best way of handling fern spores is to put pieces of the frond into a paper bag, tie the bag shut and keep in a warm room for a few days to allow the spores to be released. A fine brown or yellowish dust will accumulate in the bottom of the bag. Shake the portions of fern frond before removing them from the bag and carefully empty the spores into a storage container.

STORING SEED

If the cleaned seeds are not to be sown immediately, they must be stored in conditions that will retain their viability for the longest possible time.

Seed of some species, such as kauri (*Agathis australis*), karaka (*Corynocarpus laevigatus*) and Marlborough rock daisy (*Pachystegia* spp.), must be sown almost immediately because they soon lose their viability if stored for too long.

When storing seed the aim is to retain the maximum viability for the longest possible period. The most important requirements are a low storage temperature, low moisture content in the seed and low humidity. The optimum temperature range for storing seeds is from -1°C to 5°C. Determining the moisture content of seeds is difficult unless specialised equipment is available. Once they have been air-dried for a few days, it should be assumed that their moisture content is somewhere near the required level and they can be put into storage. Ideally, the moisture content should be within the range of 8–10%.

However, the seeds of a number of species will store quite well for a few months in open conditions without any attempt to control temperature or moisture levels. They can be put into paper envelopes in autumn and kept until sown in spring. Examples of species that can be stored in open conditions are *Acaena*, *Arthropodium*, *Carmichaelia*, *Clianthus*, *Entelea*, *Geranium*, *Leptospermum*, *Myosotis*, *Phormium*, *Viola*.

Generally, seeds that can be dry stored are better kept in air-tight containers, such as glass jars with screw-top lids, containing a desiccant. This will also protect them from mice and other pests. However, before putting the seeds into storage they should be carefully checked for any caterpillars or grubs that may already be present on them and will happily continue to eat them in storage. Two or three weeks after storing the seeds, they should again be checked for any that may have hatched from eggs. If necessary, lightly dust the seeds with an insecticide powder such as Maldison or Derris Dust. Some people prefer to routinely treat all seeds with an insecticidal dust, in which case I would recommend Derris Dust as it is the safest to use and also very effective. Dry-stored seeds can be kept in a refrigerator, either in glass containers or polythene bags. Polythene bags are permeable, allowing the contents to slowly dry out, and are better used only for short-term storage.

Seeds that will not tolerate dry storage must be kept in cool-moist storage. This is really nothing more than a form of stratification. The seeds are mixed with a moist medium, such as peat, sand, sawdust or a mixture of the three, and placed in a polythene bag, which is sealed and stored in a refrigerator until ready for sowing. The storage temperature should be 0–10°C. As with stratified seeds, about once a week the bags should be gently shaken and the mixture moistened if necessary.

6

Diseases and Pests

Anybody who propagates plants will sooner or later encounter problems in one form or another. Many can be avoided or kept to a minimum if good 'housekeeping' or hygiene measures are practised.

The old axiom which states that 'prevention is better than cure' is something which should continually be borne in mind.

All equipment and facilities should be kept as clean as possible, and pots and trays should be washed before reusing them. A solution of 1 part of bleach to 20 parts of water is ideal for this. Wash clean, leave to soak for about 15 minutes and then allow to drain dry. Wear rubber gloves to protect your hands.

The way in which facilities are managed will also help to prevent problems. In a greenhouse and other propagation structures, that means providing adequate ventilation according to the conditions and the time of year, particularly during warm humid weather. However, having the greenhouse wide open when a cold moist wind is blowing may encourage the presence of grey mould. Avoid overwatering during cold or dull weather, as this can encourage root rots and other fungal diseases.

The following are the main diseases, pests and other problems likely to be encountered by plant propagators.

DISEASES

Damping off

This is a collective term referring to several fungal diseases that all cause similar problems when raising plants from seed. It may be caused by *Phytophthora*, *Pythium*, *Rhizoctonia* or *Botrytis cinerea*. It develops suddenly and spreads very rapidly. In its most visible form it causes the seedlings to topple over, usually in groups, and when examined closely it will be observed that their stems are dark coloured and severely constricted just above soil level. Damping off occurs in several forms:

PRE-EMERGENCE DAMPING OFF: The germinating seed becomes infected, rots and dies before the seedling emerges from the medium. The spores may have been on the seed before sowing. Apart from dusting the seed with a fungicide such as Thiram and maintaining good hygiene, little can be done to prevent the attack of this disease.

POST-EMERGENCE DAMPING OFF: The seedlings develop a constriction and stem rot near the base of the stem, fall over and the whole seedling rots. As soon as it is noticed the affected area should be treated with a fungicide. Dusting with flowers of sulphur or drenching with Captan or Benlate are usually effective. Unsuitable growing conditions such as high temperatures and overwatering favour its occurrence, therefore attention should also be paid to correcting those conditions.

ROOT ROT: The rootlets of larger seedlings may be infected, causing the plants to become stunted and eventually die. The spores of this fungus are water-borne and grow rapidly at 20–30°C. The seedlings and mix should be drenched with a solution of Captan or Benlate. Growing conditions should be checked and corrected as necessary.

A biological control known as Trichopel is also very effective in preventing damping off. It is a beneficial fungus (*Trichoderma*) that discourages the growth of many soil-borne fungi. It is available in pellet form and is best used by being placed in the sowing medium adjacent to the seeds. Trichopel is now available in domestic-sized packs.

Grey mould

Botrytis cinerea is a fungus that infects a wide range of host plants. It is easily recognised by the distinctive furry greyish mould that covers the infected parts or cuttings. Often it occurs on dead or dying material such as fallen leaves, or cuttings that are failing, and then moves on to infect healthy tissue. For that reason it is important that no plant debris is allowed to accumulate in the propagation case or greenhouse. Warm humid conditions and poor ventilation favour its occurrence. Overcrowding of cuttings can also be a factor.

Spraying or drenching with Captan or Benlate will control it. At the same time attention should be paid to improving ventilation and reducing the temperature and humidity. It also attacks seedlings in the form of damping off, except that then the typical grey furriness does not appear.

Phytophthora

This is a widespread fungus that infects a very wide range of plant species and manifests itself in various ways. There are several species and collectively they are commonly known as collar rot or sometimes as root rot. They are soil-borne and high temperatures with an overwet rooting mix favour their occurrence, although depending on the species of *Phytophthora*, cold temperatures and an overwet rooting mix can also encourage its attack. Symptoms are wilting leaves that may turn brown as they die, die-back of the cutting and eventually its death. The roots and bases of cuttings are most likely to be attacked. Roots turn brownish black and lesions may develop near the base of the stem. With young seedlings it occurs in the form of damping off.

Once plants have been infected with *Phytophthora* little can be done apart from destroying all infected material and discarding the rooting mix in which the infected cuttings were planted. Drenching with a fungicide such as Captan or Benlate may possibly help to prevent its spread. Control should be aimed at prevention by not creating the conditions favoured by this disease.

Pythium

This fungus is also known as collar rot and root rot. There are several different species that may attack cuttings and and germinating seedlings. With cuttings it is generally young and soft tissue that is liable to be infected and with seedlings it causes damping off. It is most likely to occur when the rooting or seed-sowing mix is kept overly wet and it causes a progressive rotting of the softer parts of cuttings.

Immediate removal of all infected material, spraying or drenching with Captan or Benlate and correcting the conditions that caused the attack are the best means of controlling it.

Rhizoctonia

This is another fungus that causes damping off of seedlings and also attacks cuttings. Its attacks are encouraged by poor ventilation and warm humid conditions, especially during the summer. Often it will attack the young roots and can be recognised by the reddish brown colour of the infected tissue. If the surface of the rooting mix is examined closely it might be possible to see the web-like growth of the mycelia. Control measures for *Rhizoctonia* are as for the other fungal diseases.

PESTS

Fortunately few pests attack seedlings and cuttings, but those that do can on occasions be quite devastating. There are also one or two pests that can be a problem with seeds in storage.

Aphids

Occasionally aphids or greenfly are found on cuttings and more rarely on newly germinated seedlings. When they are found on cuttings it is usually because some were already present on the material when the cuttings were made. Spray with Maldison and repeat about 5–7 days later. When they attack seedlings it is possibly because a winged female has discovered the seedlings or that some were already present on nearby plants.

Often aphids will mainly attack seedlings that are under stress because their growing conditions are too dry. If they are not immediately visible on seedlings their presence is often indicated by the cotyledons and first true leaves being distorted and rolled in towards their undersurfaces. A close examination will reveal the culprits hidden in the distortions. Even one or two aphids per seedling will have a severe effect. A spray with Maldison should bring them under control but to avoid damaging the seedlings use a more dilute solution.

Mice

Mice are another pest that can cause a great amount of damage in a short space of time, especially if the propagation facility is easily accessible from outside. In the course of one night a pair of mice can go through numerous pots of newly sown seed and devour most of the seed. What they do not eat is often damaged as a result of their foraging activities. Trapping and the use of poison baits are the usual methods of control, although blocking their points of entry should not be ignored. Generally they are only a problem during autumn and early winter when outdoor conditions are becoming cooler and they are looking for warmer quarters indoors.

Slugs and snails

Of the two, slugs are probably the worst because of their ability to hide under pots, trays and similar places. Snails are generally less of a problem in indoor or protected facilities. During the course of one night one slug or snail can almost completely devour a batch of seedlings. Plastic pots with a hollow area underneath provide ready-made hiding places for slugs. A regular inspection of all likely hiding places can do a great deal towards eliminating them. If their presence is suspected a few baits should be scattered around the seedling containers. Bran-based baits are not very good because they quickly decompose and the bran becomes mouldy, thus creating another potential danger for the seedlings. Particular care should be taken to inspect any containers brought into the propagation facility from outside.

Woodlice

Woodlice or slaters have a varied diet, being both

carnivorous and herbivorous. Normally they scavenge on decaying organic matter but they also attack young seedlings, which can make them quite an important pest. In a well-maintained facility they are little trouble, but a neglected one usually provides plenty of harbouring places for them. Good hygiene is the best means of control. Keep everything clean and eliminate harbouring places, especially where seedlings are being germinated.

Caterpillars and grubs

The larvae of some native insects can be a problem in the stored seed of genera such as *Hoheria*, *Plagianthus*, *Carmichaelia*, *Notospartium* and sometimes *Sophora*. The eggs are present on the seed when it is harvested and hatch after the seed has been put into storage. The incidence of these pests varies from year to year and can be much worse in some seasons. If there is any possibility that the seed could be attacked it should be dusted with an insecticide. Derris Dust gives very good results and is a far safer product to use, especially as the seeds will later be handled when being sown. Harvesting the seed when it is still slightly green helps to avoid this problem because at that stage the insects have not usually laid their eggs.

OTHER PROBLEMS

Apart from diseases and pests, few other problems affect plant propagation, although the following can be quite troublesome.

Liverworts

Liverworts are allied to mosses and are also spore-bearing plants. The genus *Marchantia* causes problems by growing over the surface of potting and seed-sowing mixes in greenhouses, cold frames and shady places. With seed that takes a long time to germinate, liverwort can encrust the surface of the mix making it very difficult for seedlings to emerge.

With containerised plants it can similarly smother the surface of the potting mix and hinder the plant's growth.

Marchantia has a green leafy growth known as a 'thallus', which forks repeatedly and soon covers quite large areas. Moist and cool conditions favour its growth.

Control is difficult and most chemical controls are liable to damage the plants being protected. Once liverwort is present the only certain way of removing it is by hand. With containers of sown seed it must be carefully scraped off so as not to disturb the seed or germinating seedlings. When sowing seeds its occurrence can be prevented, in the short term at least, if coarse sand or fine grit is used for covering the sown seed instead of seed-sowing mix. Some growers use a layer of vermiculite instead. With any seeds that take several months to germinate, *Marchantia* will eventually make its appearance. A close watch should be kept for any thalli that appear and they should be picked off immediately. With larger-scale operations that is obviously not practicable, but on a smaller scale it can certainly keep the problem under control.

Moss

As with liverworts, mosses are mainly a problem with seeds that take several months to germinate, particularly over the winter months. Seedlings that are very slow to grow to a size convenient for handling can also be swamped by moss, which grows more quickly than the seedlings.

None of the available moss killers can be used without damaging the seedlings and so the only means of control is to remove the moss by hand. When peeling off a layer of moss from a container of seed that has not yet germinated, care must be taken that the seeds are not entangled in the moss roots and removed along with the moss. Covering sown seed with a layer of coarse sand or fine grit helps to delay the appearance of moss, but eventually it will appear.

7
Propagation of Selected Plants A–Z

Temperature conditions given for germinating seeds and rooting cuttings are as follows:

Cool	10–15°C
Intermediate	15–20°C
Warm	20–27°C

ACAENA (Biddy biddy)

SEED: Sow when ripe. Some seeds germinate within about 4 weeks and a secondary germination usually follows in the early spring. Alternatively, the seed can be stratified for 1–2 months before sowing. Germination still takes about 4 weeks. Germinate in cool to intermediate conditions. Seed usually ripens during late summer to early autumn. It stores well.

CUTTINGS: Easily propagated by tip cuttings of soft semi-hardwood stems from January until May. Rooting takes up to about 2 months.

DIVISION AND SELF-LAYERS: Species such as *A. microphylla* and *A.inermis* can be divided quite easily. Division is usually carried out in autumn or early spring. Some species are also self-layering and suitable rooted pieces can be taken off, potted and grown on.

ACIPHYLLA (Speargrass, Spaniard)

SEED: Sow when ripe, which is usually about February to March. Germinate in cool to intermediate conditions. Germination can be very erratic and may extend over 2–3 years. Alternatively, cool-moist stratify for 1–2 months and then sow in April or May. Germination should commence within 1–3 months. Seed can also be cool-moist stored for an early-spring sowing. For seeds that have been dry stored for some time, germination can be improved if they are soaked in warm water for several hours before sowing. Seed of most species ripens from late summer to autumn. It does not store well.

CUTTINGS: Some of the smaller clumping species such as *A. monroi* and *A. similis* can be propagated from cuttings. Side rosettes are carefully cut from the parent plant, surplus leaves are removed and then the rosettes inserted into a peat and sand, or peat, sand and sawdust rooting mix. Treatment with hormone will assist with rooting. It is possible to take cuttings from smaller plants of some of the larger species, but the leaves must be shortened to prevent excessive wilting. Cuttings of some species such as *A. simplex* can be rooted, but the resultant plants appear to very reluctant to make further growth. Cutting propagation is useful for raising known male and female plants or selected forms.

A. pinnatifida has a rhizomatous habit of growth and is very easily propagated by removing the rosettes that appear around the parent.

ADIANTUM (Maidenhair ferns)

SPORES: Sow according to the technique described in chapter 2. Ripe sori can be collected throughout much of the growing season. *A. diaphanum* is the easiest to propagate from spores and often self-sows with the greatest of freedom.

DIVISION: With the exception of *A. diaphanum*, which has a tufted rhizome, all species can be propagated by division. All fronds should be cut off the divisions, otherwise they only wilt and die as well as causing the divisions to lose precious moisture. To encourage good root growth, divisions should be potted into a spongy, gritty mixture and kept in a cool and shady place until new growth appears. Keep a careful watch for slugs and snails, which love the crooks or crosiers of the young fronds.

AGATHIS AUSTRALIS (Kauri)

SEED: Kauri seed loses its viability very quickly and must be sown immediately it has ripened, which is usually about late February or March. If seed cannot be sown within about 10 days of being collected, it should be held in cool-moist storage, but for no longer than is necessary. Cones collected from lone trees, or even small groups, in a garden or park situation produce very few viable seeds per cone compared with cones collected from kauri forest areas. Seedlings from the former are also considered inferior in all respects to those from the latter.

CUTTINGS AND GRAFTING: Kauri can be grown from cuttings but it is not easy and much depends on the availability of suitable cutting material. Generally, it is of little use trying shoots from reasonably large garden-grown trees because it is seldom possible to obtain good cutting material. The best cuttings are obtained from young trees that have been grown in containers for a few years and then beheaded. They usually produce a number of terminal shoots that are rather spindly in appearance. Such cuttings have a far better chance of producing roots than heavier material from an outdoor-grown tree. Time of year may also be critical as there may be just a small period when conditions are at their optimum for rooting.

It is also possible to graft selected forms onto seedling rootstocks. Side grafting is the best method to use, although some consider that top-wedge grafting is preferable. The scion must be quite dormant for the graft to be successful.

ALECTRYON EXCELSUS (Titoki)

SEED: Although titoki seed will dry store for 4–5 months, it does not store well for much longer and, generally, should be sown immediately after collection. The seeds require no pre-treatment. It can be sown with or without removing the fleshy aril. Germinate in intermediate to warm conditions. Germination can be expected after about 4 weeks or so. Seed takes 12 months to ripen, usually in the following spring, but ripening can be protracted and ripe seeds can be harvested much later than this.

ALSEUOSMIA

SEED: All species are raised from seed, but not much is known of the dormancy conditions relating to them. In general cool-moist stratification for 2–3 months is recommended. Germinate in cool to intermediate conditions. Seed of *A. pusilla* stratified for 5 months still had not germinated 5 months after sowing. Fruits of most species ripen over the summer months.

CUTTINGS: Soft semi-hardwood cuttings taken during late spring, or firm semi-hardwood cuttings taken from March to April, give the best results. Treat with hormone and root in intermediate conditions.

ANEMANTHELE LESSONIANA (Wind grass)

(syn. *Oryzopsis lessoniana*)

SEED: Easily raised from seed, which should be sown when ripe, although one grower recommends cool-moist stratification for one month before sowing. The seed is very fine and should be sown on the surface of the medium without any covering or with the merest suggestion of covering. Germinate in intermediate

conditions. Self-sown seedlings often appear around garden specimens and can be pricked out or transplanted as required. Seed usually ripens during January or February. It stores well.

DIVISION: If seed is not available, older clumps can easily be divided. In order to reduce transpiration, the foliage of divisions should be cut back by about half. Keep in a cool and shady place until new growth commences.

ANAPHALIS

SEED: Can be raised from seed, which should be sown when ripe. The seeds are quite small and should be sown on the surface of the seed-sowing mix, or according to the scree technique described in chapter 2. Germinate in cool to intermediate conditions. As with many members of the daisy family, there are often quite large numbers of infertile seeds in the seed heads. Most species have quite protracted flowering periods so that ripe seed can be harvested from November until April, according to the species. The seed does not store well.

CUTTINGS AND LAYERS: Soft semi-hardwood tip cuttings taken in February or March are not difficult to root and give good results. February cuttings usually root within 2 months and those taken in March may take longer. The various species layer quite easily and self-layered stems can often be found on plants.

ANISOTOME

SEED: Most species are raised from seed, which should be given cool-moist stratification for 1–2 months before sowing. Depending on species and locality, seeds may ripen from November until April. Seed sown in April takes about 1 month to germinate, in May about 2 months and in August 2–12 months. Some of the high-alpine species can take 12 months or more to germinate. Seed should be given cool conditions for germination. If seed has been kept in dry storage for some time, germination is improved if the seeds are soaked in warm water for several hours before sowing.

DIVISION: *Anisotome* plants usually have one to several large taproots, which makes it very difficult to divide mature plants. Younger plants with more than one crown can be divided by carefully cutting off one of the side crowns with a piece of the root system attached. The cut surfaces should be dusted with a fungicide such as Thiram or Captan to prevent rot from occurring. The foliage must be cut back by half to prevent the division from collapsing. Pot the division into a gritty medium to encourage new root growth and keep in cool shady conditions.

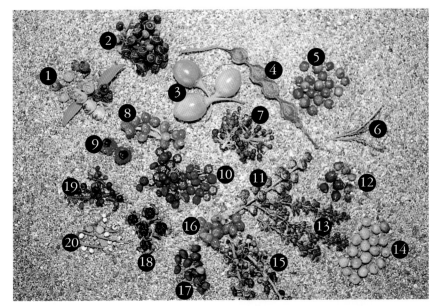

Key to Fruits
  1. Metrosideros umbellata, *southern rata*
  2. Carpodetus serratus, *putaputaweta*
  3. Solanum laciniatum, *poroporo*
  4. Sophora microphylla, *kowhai*
  5. Corokia cotoneaster, *red-fruited form*
  6. Carex devia, *sedge*
  7. Melicytus ramiflorus, *mahoe*
  8. Coprosma lucida, *karangu*
  9. Alectryon excelsus, *titoki*
  10. Cyathodes juniperina, *mingimingi*
  11. Leptospermum scoparium, *manuka*
  12. Gaultheria antipoda, *snowberry*
  13. Kunzea ericoides, *kanuka*
  14. Corokia cotoneaster, *yellow-fruited form*
  15. Schefflera digitata, *pate*
  16. Coprosma robusta, *karamu*
  17. Griselinia littoralis, *broadleaf*
  18. Pittosporum tenuifolium, *kohuhu*
  19. Myrsine australis, *mapou*
  20. Melicytus alpinus, *porcupine bush*

Recently germinated tawa (Beilschmiedia tawa) *seedlings. Note how the seed was only partially buried.*

Flower and seeds of Rhopalostylis sapida, *nikau*

Fruits of Coprosma rhamnoides

Fruits of Coprosma brunnea

Seeds of Pittosporum crassifolium, *karo*

Seed heads of Acaena microphylla

Fruits of Gaultheria antipoda

Above: Lifting a seedling from its seedling punnet. Note how the dibber is used to lift the seedling from underneath.

Above, right: After making a hole in the mix with the dibber drop the seedling's roots into it.

Right: When the tray is full, tidy the surface of the mix by quickly running the dibber between the rows of plants.

Left, above: Kanuka (Kunzea ericoides) seedlings shortly after germination, which took 14 days. The seed could have been sown more thinly.

Left, below: Seedlings of Myosotis capitata. The seed was scattered among the stone chips according to the scree technique.

Fruits of Dacrycarpus dacrydioides, *kahikatea or white pine*

Seeds of Carmichaelia aligera, *native broom*

Fruits of Astelia fragrans, *kahakaha*

Seed heads of Clematis paniculata

Seed pods of Phormium cookianum

Seed head of Bulbinella rossii

Sophora tetraptera, *kowhai, seeds and buds*

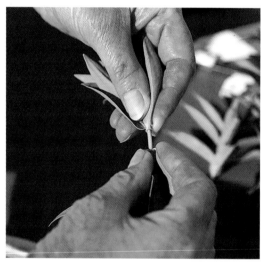

Top: Young Hebe *plants in fibre pots ready for potting on. Note the dry areas on the fibre pots. These plants should be soaked in water before being put into their new pots.*

Above: Potting on. Position the plant at the correct depth, in the centre of the pot, and add more potting mix.

Left, top to bottom: Making cuttings, use secateurs to remove a cutting from a branch taken off the parent plant. Strip off the surplus foliage by holding the thumb and first three fingers around the stem. Insert the prepared cutting into the rooting mix.

Coprosma x kirkii *'Kirkii' cuttings showing the percentages using different hormones. Left to right: control (no treatment), 40%; Seradix 1, 80%; Seradix 2, 60%; Seradix 3, 100%; Clonex, 100%*

Rooted cuttings of tauhinu (Cassinia leptophylla) *and* Olearia serpentina. *Note the difference between the root systems of the two species. For the nature of the plant, the* Olearia *cuttings are really quite well rooted.*

A small plant of Astelia fragrans *sliced open to show the position of the basal plate. Its outline can be discerned extending in a dome shape from one side of the brown area to the other.*

Left, above: A 1-year-old plant of cabbage tree (Cordyline australis) *showing the 'toe' just commencing to form. When it is a little longer it can be removed and treated as a root cutting.*

Left: Induced branching of Astelia. *The first growths have emerged from A. fragrans 6 weeks after the tops have been cut off at the basal plate.*

An example of a grafted standard Hebe. *In this instance* H. 'Hartii' *has been side grafted onto a tall rootstock of* H. barkeri.

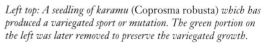

Left top: A seedling of karamu (Coprosma robusta) *which has produced a variegated sport or mutation. The green portion on the left was later removed to preserve the variegated growth.*

Left centre: Liverwort (Marchantia) *just commencing to infest a tray of* Libertia *seedlings.*

Left: Seedlings of totorowhiti (Dracophyllum strictum) *being threatened by a thick growth of moss. The seed was sown in January 1993 and took almost 2 years to germinate.*

APIUM (New Zealand celery)

SEED: Easily raised from seed, which should be sown when fresh. The germination of older seed can be improved by soaking it in warm water for several hours before sowing. Germinate in cool to intermediate conditions. The seed ripens from about January to April and probably has a storage life of about 12 months.

DIVISION AND LAYERS: Older plants can either be divided or propagated by self-rooted layers that are sometimes freely produced.

ARISTOTELIA (Wineberry or mako mako)

SEED: Both *A. fruticosa* and *A. serrata* are usually raised from seed, which should be given cool-moist stratification for 1–2 months before sowing. Germinate in cool to intermediate conditions. Germination takes about 2 months or so. As soon as they ripen the fruits are often quickly eaten by birds and it may be preferable to collect slightly immature fruits, than to make daily trips to collect ripe ones. Seed ripens between January and April. It stores well.

CUTTINGS: Selected forms of both species and the hybrid *A.* x *fruserrata* can be propagated from cuttings. Softwood, semi-hardwood or hardwood cuttings will all strike, although semi-hardwood cuttings taken in March probably give the best results. Rooting can take up to about 2 months.

ARTHROPODIUM (Rock lily, renga renga)

SEED: Both species (*A. cirratum and A. candidum*) are easily propagated from seed. *A. candidum* 'Rubrum' will come true from seed, provided the seed has not been collected from a plant growing near the typical *A. candidum*. Generally, seed should be sown when fresh but it will dry store for 12 months or longer without losing much viability. Germinate in intermediate to warm conditions. Germination usually takes about 1 month. The seed should be sown rather thinly because the young seedlings are sometimes susceptible to attack from *Botrytis*. Slugs and snails are very fond of the seedlings. Seed ripens between January and February.

DIVISION: Selected forms of *A. cirratum* are easily propagated by division during spring. Two forks should be used for making the divisions so as not to cause too much damage to the fleshy roots and the foliage should be cut back quite severely. Both *A. candidum* and its cultivar produce numerous tubers and clumps can be divided in spring as the new foliage appears. They also produce masses of self-sown seedlings.

ASPLENIUM

SPORES: All species can be propagated from spores. Sow according to the technique described in chapter 2. Ripe sori can be collected from most species during most of the growing season.

GEMMAE OR PLANTLETS: In New Zealand the hen and chickens fern (*A. bulbiferum*) is propagated almost exclusively by the bulbils or plantlets that develop on its older fronds (see chapter 4 for details). On the fronds of the necklace fern (*A. flabellifolium*) the midrib is sometimes extended for several centimetres beyond the pinnae and on its tip a solitary bulbil is produced. When it touches the ground it takes root and grows into a new plant. Once rooted the new plant can be removed and transplanted.

DIVISION: The majority of *Asplenium* species can be divided if crowns are carefully removed from the sides of clumps with a few roots attached. The fronds should be cut off, leaving only short lengths of the stalks or stipites attached. Pot the divisions and keep in a cool humid atmosphere until new growth is well established. *A. flabellifolium* is very easily divided.

ASTELIA

SEED: All species are propagated from seed but cultivars and selected forms such as male and female plants must be propagated vegetatively. The seed should be cleaned and sown when fresh, or it can be cool-moist stratified for 1–2 months before sowing. Germination usually commences in late winter or early spring, although sometimes it may take up to 12 months. Fruits of some species ripen between January and May, but *A. solandri* flowers and fruits for much of the year. *A. trinervia* also has a long fruiting season from July to May. The seed stores well.

DIVISION: Division of clumps can be carried out in early spring. It is preferable not to make the divisions too small unless a large number of plants are desired. The foliage should be cut back to about one-third before the divisions are potted. Branching of young plants can be mechanically induced so that they can be divided at a later date (see chapter 4). This is a very good technique for quickly building up stocks of particular cultivars or forms.

AVICENNIA RESINIFERA (Mangrove)

SEED: Sow immediately after gathering. Plant the seeds in plastic drink bottles that have had their necks cut off and filled with mud or muddy sand taken from an estuary. Cover the mud with 5–10 mm of sea water and just lay the seeds on the surface. Germinate in intermediate to warm conditions. The seeds will tolerate full sun. Germination should commence within 24 hours and within a week the seedling should be standing erect with the first two leaves visible. Maintain at least 5 mm of water on the surface. Use sea water or salty water (30 g salt per litre = sea water strength) alternating with fresh water. Fresh water is important if plants are being kept indoors. When ready for transplanting, cut away the plastic bottle carefully because the roots are very sensitive to damage. Transplant into a wide container with plenty of room for the roots to spread outwards and for the pneumatophores (breathing roots) to grow upwards. At this stage the mortality rate can be quite high and twice as many seedlings as required should be transplanted. Seed ripens throughout summer and autumn and has a very short viability. Seed should be harvested from the tree because fallen seed that has already germinated is much more difficult to establish.

BEILSCHMIEDIA (Tawa, taraire)

SEED: Tawa and taraire seeds soon lose their viability and should be sown when fresh, or they can be cool-moist stored for 1 month before sowing. Seed usually ripens during late summer and can be gathered off the ground beneath parent trees. Unlike most plants with fleshy fruits it is not necessay to clean the flesh off the seeds before sowing. The seeds are large and it is preferable to individually space them when sowing as it makes later handling much easier. Many growers just lightly press the seeds into the seed-sowing mix so that they are only half-buried. Alternatively, they can be lightly covered. The former is the preferred method and germination is often about 100%. Germination occurs quite well in cool to intermediate conditions. The first seedlings normally appear within about 2 months, with the balance continuing to germinate over a period of time after that. The seeds and germinating seedlings can rot easily and care must be taken not to over-water them.

BLECHNUM (Hard ferns)

SPORES: All species can be propagated from spores. Sow according to the technique described in chapter 2. Species such as *B. discolor* and *B. filiforme* often produce ripe sori at different times during the growing season, while those of species such as *B. pennamarina* and *B. fluviatile* often only ripen during mid-summer.

DIVISION: Species that produce multiple crowns (e.g., *B.minus*), rhizomes (e.g., *B. filiforme* and *B. pennamarina*) or stolons (*B. discolor*) can have rooted divisions taken off them. When dividing *B. pennamarina* it is not usually necessary to cut off the fronds from the divisions, but the fronds of other species should be reduced in length to about one-quarter. *B. filiforme* occurs in two distinct forms. When it grows on the ground it has short fronds, but when it

commences to climb a tree they become very much longer and more graceful. Providing care is taken to select a well-rooted portion of the ground form it is not too difficult to propagate, but the climbing form is quite difficult. For this form, take a length of rhizome, fasten it to a suitable growing medium such as a tree-fern trunk, pack some moss around the rhizome and keep it in a very humid atmosphere until it takes root and growth commences. The fronds should be shortened but not completely cut off.

BRACHYGLOTTIS

With 30 species and quite a large number of cultivars, both named and unnamed, it is not possible to individually discuss the propagation of each one.

SEED: All species can be propagated from seed, which should be sown as soon as ripe. If necessary, seed can be dry stored for several weeks at 4–10°C without the viability being affected. Seed can also be held in cool-moist storage for 4–5 months and sown in spring. Depending on conditions, germination takes 2–4 weeks, although with some species it can take longer and could be somewhat erratic. Germinate in intermediate conditions. In some seasons seed heads contain a large number of sterile seeds so that it may be necessary to sow a large quantity in order to obtain a few seedlings. Seed of most species ripens from about January to March.

CUTTINGS: All woody species, hybrids and cultivars are easily propagated from semi-hardwood or hardwood cuttings, which are generally best taken during March and April. Root in cool to intermediate conditions. Cuttings usually take 2–6 months to root and there is normally a good strike rate. Species such as *B. rotundifolia*, which has thicker stems, can be a bit more difficult and take longer to root. Similarly, alpine species such as *B. bifistulosa*, which only make short annual growth, can also be difficult because cuttings of suitable length usually comprise much hardwood. Plants of the 'repanda' group have very large leaves and each leaf must be reduced in size to about half or less. Species such as *B. compacta*, *B. greyi*, *B. perdicioides* and the various cultivars of the Dunedin Hybrids group can also be propagated from long hardwood cuttings set out in the open ground. These cuttings should be 20–30 cm long and taken between late May and early June. Rooting occurs during the summer and by the following winter some will have grown into plants large enough to be planted in permanent positions; the remainder should be lined out for growing on.

DIVISION: Some herbaceous species (e.g. *B. haastii*) can be propagated by division, but others form only single rosettes and must be propagated from seed.

BRACHYSCOME

SEED: Only one species, *B. sinclairii*, is at all commonly cultivated. Seed should be sown when ripe and treated as for other members of the daisy family. Sowing according to the scree technique is a good way of ensuring success. Seed ripens between December and March. It stores reasonably well.

DIVISION: When plants are large enough they are easily propagated by division.

BULBINELLA (Golden star lily or Maori onion)

SEED: All species are easily raised from seed, which should be cool-moist stratified for 3 months before sowing. Germinate in cool conditions. Seed ripens during late summer and early autumn. It stores well.

DIVISION: Plants of *Bulbinella* are easily divided just as growth is about to commence in the spring. Usually the clumps are not difficult to separate by hand, but if difficulty is experienced use two hand forks to separate them. For the best results divisions should have at least 3–4 crowns. Replant divisions as soon as possible.

CALDCLUVIA ROSIFOLIA (Makamaka)
(syn. *Ackama rosifolia*)

SEED: Generally raised from seed. Sow when ripe or cool-moist stratify for 2 months before sowing. Germinate in intermediate or warm conditions. The seed stores reasonably well.

CUTTINGS: Can also be propagated from semi-hardwood cuttings taken during April. Root in intermediate conditions. The use of hormone is recommended.

CAREX

SEED: All species can be propagated from seed. Sow when ripe, although the germination of some species is hastened and improved if the seed is cool-moist stratified for 1 month before sowing. Germinate in cool conditions. Depending on the species germination can take from 1–7 months and can be erratic. Seed of most species ripens between February and May. The seed stores well.

DIVISION: Carexes divide easily and, as with grasses, the foliage of divisions must be shortened by about half. Division is best carried out in spring, although some species can be divided at almost any time during the growing season.

CARMICHAELIA (Native brooms)

SEED: Seed keeps for many years in dry storage (see chapter 2, Seed Dormancy). Give freshly collected seeds hot-water treatment (50°C) before sowing. The water temperature for older seed should be 70–90°C. Cool-moist stratification for 1–2 months before sowing also aids germination. Germinate in intermediate conditions. Germination will usually take about 3 weeks, but if seed is sown during winter germination can be up to 6 weeks. Seed of *C. williamsii* has been known to commence germination in the pod. Seed of most species ripens between February and April. It stores well.

CUTTINGS: Firm semi-hardwood or hardwood cuttings of most species root quite easily. They can be taken all year round and rooting usually takes from 1–12 months, according to species and time of year. Hardwood cuttings of *C. astonii* taken in late October rooted within 6 weeks. Rather than trying to make properly trimmed cuttings it is often better to just tear the cutting off the branch so that it comes away with a heel. Do not try to trim smooth the whole heel, but simply tidy the ragged stringy bits at the lower end of the heel. This particularly applies to species that have broad and heavy branchlets. The use of hormones is advisable. Root in intermediate conditions. Small matted species such as *C. enysii* can also be propagated by removing branchlets with a few roots attached.

CARPODETUS SERRATUS (Putaputaweta)

SEED: Sow when fresh or cool-moist stratify for 6–8 weeks. Germination can take up to 2 months or more and there is usually a very good germination rate. The efficacy of stratification or other treatments to break dormancy have yet to be determined. Seed that was leached, then stratified for 4 months and sown in September still did not germinate until 2 months later. Germinating seedlings can be very susceptible to *Pythium*. Seed usually ripens from February to May. It stores well.

CUTTINGS: Semi-hardwood cuttings should be taken during March or April. Root in intermediate conditions. Treat with hormone.

CASSINIA (Tauhinu, cottonwood)

SEED: Easily raised from seed if genetic diversity is required for environmental plantings otherwise plants are usually propagated by cuttings. Germinate in intermediate conditions. Germination takes about 1 month. Stores reasonably well.

CUTTINGS: Semi-hardwood or hardwood cuttings root quite easily and can be taken over much of the year. The soft growing tips should be removed. Hormone treatment is not necessary but hastens rooting. Root in cool to intermediate conditions. Rooting takes 2–5 months according to the time of year and the condition of the cutting material. Long hardwood cuttings taken during late May or early June can also be rooted in the open ground.

CELMISIA (Mountain daisy)

SEED: Seed sown as soon as it has ripened often germinates readily and within 4–6 weeks. Some growers prefer to cool-moist stratify the seed for 4–8 weeks before sowing. Older seed requires a period of low temperature and should be stratified before sowing. Stratified seed may take up to 8 weeks to germinate. *Celmisia* seed soon loses its viability and after about 8 weeks storage, viability declines rapidly. Sowing according to the scree technique gives very good results, however some growers prefer to sow the seed on the surface of the medium and barely cover it. Germination occurs best at cooler temperatures, preferably at 10–15°C, but 5–15°C is tolerable. Darkness tends to retard or inhibit germination and, apart from shading from direct sunlight, containers should be kept in a well-lit situation. Seed collected from wild plants often contains a high percentage of infertile seeds (sometimes up to 96%) due to fungal infection, predation by insects or just poor pollination, whereas that collected from cultivated plants often has a much higher percentage of viable seeds. Some species regularly produce good crops of fertile seed in most years. If conditions are not suitable, newly germinated seedlings can be susceptible to damping off. Slugs and snails also have a fondness for them. Seed of most species ripens between January and April.

CUTTINGS: Cuttings of the subshrubby species such as *C. walkeri, C. angustifolia* and *C. brevifolia* can be rooted without too much difficulty. Semi-hardwood tip cuttings taken between March and May take 2–8 months to root. Root in cool to intermediate conditions. Treatment with hormones aids the rooting process.

DIVISION: Rosette species such as *C. semicordata, C. monroi, C. gracilenta, C. holosericea* and *C. mackaui* can be propagated by division. Clumps should be lifted in spring with as much root as possible and some of the smaller side rosettes carefully removed from the parent. With some species it may be necessary to use a knife to separate them. As long as each rosette has some roots attached there should be no problem with getting them to grow. *C. holosericea* is one of the easiest to divide and often it is only necessary to tear rosettes off the parent plant. Its divisions can either be potted or in cooler areas lined out in the open ground for growing on.

CHIONOCHLOA

SEED: Sow when ripe. Sow the seed on the surface and do not cover or apply just the merest suggestion of a covering. The seeds are light sensitive and should be germinated in well-lit conditions, only providing shade from direct sunlight. Some growers prefer to cool-moist stratify the seed for 1 month before sowing.

Fresh seed will germinate within about 10 days, but depending on conditions it can take from 1–4 months. Seed can be held in dry storage (4–10°C) for up to 6 months without impairing viability too much. Depending on the species and district, seed usually ripens from the beginning of January to mid-February. It is quickly dispersed.

DIVISION: All tussock-forming species are easily propagated by division. Divisions should comprise several tillers and not be too small. Single tillers can be used but it takes much longer for them to grow into reasonable plants. The foliage of divisions should be cut back to about half of its length. Divisions of the mat-forming carpet grass (*C. australis*) are not particularly easy to establish.

CHIONOHEBE

SEED: Sow when ripe or cool-moist stratify and sow in early spring. It is best sown using the scree technique. Germinate in cool to intermediate conditions. Seed usually ripens from about February to April. It stores well.

DIVISION: Most species are cushion-forming plants and small divisions can be carefully taken from the lower sides of the cushions. They should be potted into a gritty medium to help them become established. *C. densiflora* is a small sprawling plant that does not form cushions. It can be propagated either from rooted divisions or cuttings.

CHORDOSPARTIUM (Weeping brooms)

SEED: Both species are easily raised from seed, which should be sown when fresh. If the seed is sown as soon as harvested no treatment is necessary, but older seed should be given hot-water treatment (50°C followed by soaking for 12 hours) before sowing. Germinate in intermediate conditions. Seeds usually ripen about March and store well.

CHRISTELLA DENTATA

SPORES: This species is easily raised from spores. Sow according to the technique described in chapter 2.

DIVISION: Rooted divisions are easily taken off the creeping rhizome. Cut off the fronds from the divisions, or just leave the lowest few pairs of pinnae on the fronds. Pot the divisions and keep in a humid atmosphere until new growth is well established.

CLEMATIS

All species are propagated from seed, but cultivars, selected forms and plants of known sex must be propagated from cuttings.

SEED: Either sow immediately after ripening or cool-moist stratify for 1–2 months before sowing. Older seed is probably best stratified before sowing. Germination can take 2–7 months. Seed of *C. foetida* dry stored for 1 month and sown in late December germinated 6 months later with an almost 100% result. *C. marmoraria* seed sown in March took 7 months to germinate. Other growers have found that *Clematis* seed can be somewhat erratic and may germinate over 2–3 years. It is not necessary to clean the seeds and the persistent feathery styles can be left attached. Seed of most species usually ripens between November and February. The seed stores well.

CUTTINGS: All forms can be propagated from semi-hardwood cuttings taken in February or March. Cuttings taken during October, when many of the species are in flower, will also root quite well. It is an easy way to determine which are male and female plants. Tip cuttings of some species will root quite successfully but most are better from firmer stem cuttings. Internodal cuttings are successful but stem cuttings taken with a node at the base and another at the top are probably best.

CLIANTHUS PUNICEUS (Kaka beak)

SEED: The red-flowered *C. puniceus* and the cultivars 'Albus' and 'Roseus' are all easily propagated from seed, although the latter can show some variation of flower colour. The seeds are usually given hot-water treatment before sowing but, as their seed coats are not as hard as those of *Sophora*, the water should not be near boiling point; about 50–60°C should be sufficient. Newly ripened seed treated with hot water (50°C and soak for 24 hours) germinated within 10 days and untreated seed germinated within 15 days. Cool-moist stratification for 2 months is also said to be effective in germinating *Clianthus* seed. Depending on conditions and treatment, germination can take up to 4 weeks. The seed usually ripens from about January to February. It stores well.

CUTTINGS: A number of different clones are in cultivation and should be propagated from cuttings as they may not come true from seed. Semi-hardwood cuttings root quite easily. Cuttings taken during October and November take about 3 months to root and can have a strike rate of up to 95%.

COLENSOA PHYSALOIDES (Roru)
(syn. *Pratia physaloides*)

SEED: Seed should be sown as soon as ripe.

Germination is better if the temperature is around 16–20°C; below that the germination percentage may not be very high. Seed usually ripens between October and March. It stores well.

CUTTINGS: Can be propagated from both softwood and semi-hardwood cuttings. Root in intermediate conditions and treat with hormone. Semi-hardwood cuttings taken during October take about 3 months to root and have a very good strike rate.

COLLOSPERMUM HASTATUM (Kahakaha)

SEED: Generally propagated from seed, which should be treated as for *Astelia*. Seed ripens from March to August.

DIVISION: Easily propagated by division of the clumps. Refer to *Astelia* for the technique.

COPROSMA

SEED: Sow when fresh. A 2–3 month period of cool-moist stratification is usually recommended, however the benefits of stratification are by no means proven. For example, stratified seed of *C. robusta* sown in September took 1 month for the first seedling to appear, but germination of most seedlings was not completed until over 2 months later. Stratified seed of *C. ciliata*, sown at the same time, did not begin to germinate for 3 months.

Untreated seed of *C. robusta* and *C. rotundifolia* sown in March, as soon as it had been collected, germinated the following August. Leaching has been tried on one or two species but does not appear to make any difference. Seed sown in April took about 4 months to germinate. Other growers have found that most species germinate readily, but that some species (e.g. *C. spathulata*) can germinate over a 2–3 year period.

The fruits of most species ripen from March to May, but ripe fruits are sometimes found on *C. grandifolia* during early summer. *Coprosma* seed does not keep particularly well in dry storage.

CUTTINGS: Semi-hardwood and hardwood cuttings can all be used for propagating coprosmas. Cuttings can be taken over quite a long period with March to May being the best months, however they can also be taken right through until August. Cuttings taken during March and April took 2–6 months to root and those taken in August rooted within 4 months. The foliage of the larger-leaved species needs to be reduced in size.

DIVISION: Some species such as *C. petriei*, *C. atropurpurea* and *C. pumila* can also be propagated by rooted divisions, which are easily removed from the parent plant.

CORDYLINE (Cabbage or ti trees)

SEED: Seed can be sown when ripe (February to March) and will take about 2 months to germinate, or it can be cool-moist stratified for 1 month and then sown. Results can be variable and stratified seed can germinate within 1 month or more. *C. australis* 'Purpurea' will come true from seed providing it is not growing where it can be pollinated by typical *C. australis*, but there may be some slight variation in the colour of the foliage. Plants grown as *C. banksii* 'Purpurea' are of hybrid origin (*C. banksii* x *C. australis* 'Purpurea') and seed-raised plants will be variable. Seed of most species ripens between January and May, and often remains on the plant for some time after ripening. *C. kaspar* seed ripens during April and May. *Cordyline* seed stores well and will keep for 12 months or more in dry storage at 12–15°C.

CUTTINGS: Selected forms of *C. banksii*, *C. pumilio* and some *C. pumilio* hybrids can be propagated from hardwood stem sections (refer to chapter 4). All cordylines can be propagated from 'toes', which are a kind of root cutting (refer to chapter 4). For many cultivars it is really the only practical method. For this technique to be successful it is necessary to propagate from young plants. Treatment of cuttings with hormones is recommended.

DIVISION: Both *C. pumilio* and *C.* 'Ti Tawhiti' can be propagated from rooted divisions taken off the parent plant. The latter is an old Maori cultivar and division is the only means of propagating it. Other cultivars can be propagated by the same technique providing plants can be induced to stool from below ground level. *C. australis* 'Albertii' is one which is propagated in this way as well as from 'toes'.

CORIARIA (Tutu)

SEED: Usually sown when fresh. Germination is variable and can take 9–12 months, but seed sown in May can germinate within 1 month. One grower suggests dry storage for 2 months will shorten the germination time. Fruits of the various species generally ripen from January to April, although much earlier ripening has been recorded for some species. The seed stores well.

DIVISION: The smaller species, which have creeping rhizomes, can be propagated by taking individual stems with pieces of rooted rhizome attached.

COROKIA (Korokio)

SEED: Sow when fresh or cool-moist stratify for 2–3 months before sowing. Germination is slow and can take up to 12 months. Stratification alone has little effect on germination. One grower recommends scarifying the seeds, followed by 1–2 months of cool-moist stratification before sowing. *Corokia* seeds are produced in a fleshy, berry-like fruit known as a drupe. The fruits ripen in autumn (March to May) and on cultivated plants sometimes remain until July. The seed stores well.

CUTTINGS: All corokias propagate readily from cuttings and for cultivars of the *C.* x *virgata* group it is the only method. Firm semi-hardwood and hardwood cuttings are the preferred kinds . Cuttings of *C. buddleioides* are slower to strike and can take up to 8 months to root, but cuttings of other species taken during August to November take 3–4 months to root and have good rooting percentages. Hardwood cuttings of *C. cotoneaster* taken in April rooted within 2 months.

CORTADERIA (Toe toe)

SEED: Usually the seed is sown when fresh, although cool-moist stratification for 1 month before sowing is said to improve germination. Fresh seed sown in March germinated within 20 days. Seed should be left uncovered or barely covered. Germinate in intermediate conditions. Seed normally ripens during January and February and disperses quite quickly. It stores well.

DIVISION: *Cortaderia* is easily propagated by division, which can be carried out at any time from autumn until early spring. Divisions of single tillers are quite successful, although several tillers together make better plants more quickly. Cut back the foliage by at least half.

CORYNOCARPUS LAEVIGATUS (Karaka)

SEED: Seed should be sown when fresh. Germination takes up to 6 months depending on conditions. These large seeds should be sown individually and either pressed into the sowing mix with a float before covering or partially buried as is done with *Beilschmiedia*. For large-scale production, placing the seeds individually in cell trays is a convenient way to handle them. Germinate in intermediate to warm conditions.

It is recommended that sown seeds be given an insecticidal drench to prevent infestation by a species of small maggot. Seedlings are deep-rooting and should be grown in deep containers. Variegated cultivars must always be propagated vegetatively. *Corynocarpus* fruits ripen in late summer or early autumn. The seed does not store well.

CUTTINGS: Semi-hardwood cuttings can be rooted but are often difficult. Soft semi-hardwood cuttings might be preferable to firm semi-hardwood cuttings and all available hormones should be tried. Bottom heat would also be an aid to rooting. Reduce the leaf size when making cuttings.

GRAFTING: In the past, side grafting onto seedling rootstocks has been used for propagating the variegated cultivars but nowadays does not appear to be much used. Some variegated cultivars are rather slow of growth and, as well as not always producing good cutting wood, can be difficult from cuttings. For cultivars such as *C. laevigatus* 'Moonlight' and *C. laevigatus* 'Variegatus' it is still a useful method of propagation.

CRASPEDIA

SEED: All species are easily raised from seed, which should be sown when fresh. It can be sown normally, but the preferred method is the scree technique. Germinate in cool to intermediate conditions. Germination usually takes about 10 days. Slugs and snails are very fond of the seedlings. Ripe seed is usually obtainable from late January until late April. The seed does not store well.

DIVISION: All species that produce more than one crown or rosette are easily divided. Divisions should be potted into a well-drained gritty mix until they are well established. They are prone to attack by wilt diseases.

CYATHEA (Tree ferns)

SPORES: All species are easily propagated from spores. Sow according to the technique described in chapter 2. Ripe sori can usually be collected at various times throughout the growing season, although spring is the best time.

CYATHODES

SEED: All species can be propagated from seeds but they are considered difficult. Germinate in cool to intermediate conditions. Germination is variable and can take up to 3 years. It is not yet known whether stratification makes any real difference. According to the species, ripe fruits are generally present on plants from January until April or May. Ripe fruits can be found on *C. fraseri* from as early as November. The seeds store well.

CUTTINGS: *Cyathodes* species can be propagated from cuttings but they are difficult and not a great deal is known about them. Softwood or soft semi-hardwood cuttings probably offer the best chance of success, and as well as experimenting with the various hormones cuttings should be tried with the growing tips removed. The time of year could also be important. Semi-hardwood cuttings of *C. fraseri* taken during April can take 9 months to root.

DIVISION: Lower-growing species such as *C. fraseri* can also be propagated by removing rooted divisions. After removal, the divisions need to be treated carefully and kept in a cool shady situation until they have become established.

DACRYCARPUS DACRYDIOIDES (Kahikatea or white pine)

SEED: Not too difficult to raise from seed, which is generally sown when fresh. The seeds are black and sit on top of an orange or orange-scarlet fleshy receptacle (aril). They usually ripen from March to May. Germination takes 2–4 months. The young seedlings are susceptible to damping off. The seed stores reasonably well.

CUTTINGS: Cuttings are used to bypass the juvenile phase and produce plants of adult form. Opinions vary concerning the best kind of of cuttings to use. One grower recommends hardwood cuttings taken in March, whereas another grower recommends semi-hardwood cuttings. Whichever kind is chosen, care should be taken to select only those growths that show apical dominance and will grow into an erect tree.

DACRYDIUM CUPRESSINUM (Rimu)

SEED: This species is mainly propagated from seed. It should be cool-moist stratified for 3 months before sowing and germinated in cool conditions. The seed is usually ripe from about late autumn until mid-winter. It stores reasonably well.

CUTTINGS: Cuttings are rather difficult and slow to root. Semi-hardwood and hardwood cuttings taken during mid-winter offer the best chance of success. As with *Dacrycarpus*, care should be taken to use wood that is apically dominant.

DAMNAMENIA VERNICOSA

SEED: Seed propagation is as for *Celmisia*.

DIVISION: Older plants of *D. vernicosa* can often be propagated by division. Leafy runners are sent out and usually produce new rosettes at their tips. The rosettes may or may not root in. They are easily taken off as divisions if they have already rooted, or treated as cuttings in the absence of roots.

DAVALLIA TASMANII

SPORES: Sow according to the technique described in chapter 2. Ripe sori can usually be collected throughout the growing season.

DIVISION: Rooted sections of the rhizome bearing one or two fronds can be taken. Pot into a spongy gritty mix, cut back the fronds to reduce their total area and keep in moist shady conditions until new growth is well established.

DEPARIA PETERSENII

SPORES: Sow according to the technique described in chapter 2. Ripe sori are produced for much of the year. Self-sown sporelings often come up with great abundance around plants of this species.

DIVISION: Rooted divisions can be removed from the creeping rhizome. See *Davallia* for treatment.

DESMOSCHOENUS SPIRALIS (Pingao)

SEED: Mainly propagated from seed, which should be sown when fresh. One grower recommends cool-moist stratification for 1 month before sowing. Germinate in cool to intermediate conditions. Germination can be erratic. Seed usually ripens during late summer and throughout autumn. It stores well.

DIVISION: *Desmoschoenus* can also be propagated by taking rooted divisions off the creeping rhizome. Divisions can be planted directly into the garden or put into containers. Reduce the length of the foliage before planting.

DICKSONIA (Tree ferns)

SPORES: Sow according to the technique described in chapter 2. The best time for collecting ripe sori is during early spring before drying spring winds cause them to burst open, although spores can also be collected during other times of the year. *D. fibrosa* and the trunked form of *D. lanata* can only be propagated from spores.

DIVISION: *D. squarrosa* and the trunkless form of *D. lanata* both produce stolons and can be propagated by division. The stolons usually arise close to the parent plant and once the crown has emerged and produced one or two fronds it can be severed from the parent. These divisions can be planted directly into the garden or grown on in pots for later planting out. *D. squarrosa* produces adventitious buds along its trunk. If a freshly cut trunk is laid on the ground or half-buried in the ground, where it is suitably damp, the buds will sprout into growth and that part of the trunk will eventually root into the ground. Those growing sections can later be removed and transplanted.

DIPLAZIUM AUSTRALE

SPORES: Sow according to the technique described in chapter 2. Ripe sori are produced on the plant for much of the year. Self-sown sporelings often come up with great abundance around this plant.

DISPHYMA (Horokaka)

SEED: Easily raised from seed, which is best sown when fresh. Germinate in intermediate conditions. Ripe seed capsules are generally produced from late spring until autumn. The seed keeps well in storage.

CUTTINGS: Softwood and soft semi-hardwood cuttings root very easily. They can be used for propagating selected colour forms. The plant readily self-layers, which can also be used for producing new plants.

DODONAEA VISCOSA (Ake ake)

SEED: Sow when fresh and germinate in intermediate to warm conditions. Germination usually occurs fairly quickly. One grower recommends cool-moist stratification for 4–6 weeks before sowing. Ripe seed can usually be harvested from late December until February. It stores well. Both the typical green-leaved form and the purple-leaved cultivar are propagated from seed. Seed of *D. viscosa* 'Purpurea' should be collected only from plants that are true to type and growing where they cannot cross with other forms. Harvesting of seed from plants that are not true to type is unfortunately resulting in many poor forms being grown.

CUTTINGS: Semi-hardwood cuttings can be used for propagating selected clones and is the only method for the variegated *D. viscosa* 'Moonbeam'.

DOLICHOGLOTTIS

SEED: Seed should be cool-moist stratified and sown in early spring. After sowing cover with a layer of 10 mm stone chips or coarse sand that has had the fines sifted out. Seed normally ripens during January and February.

DIVISION: *D. lyallii* is not too difficult to divide providing the side growths are carefully removed with some root attached. Reduce the length of the foliage and keep in a cool shady place until new growth commences. *D. scorzoneroides* is less inclined to form clumps and being more difficult to cultivate it is not so easily divided.

DONATIA NOVAE-ZELANDIAE

SEED: Cool-moist stratify the seed for 3 months before sowing. Sow according to the scree technique, as described in chapter 2, and germinate in cool conditions. Ripe seed may be found on plants from January until March. The seed capsules are more or less sunk into the cushions and are difficult to collect. A pair of tweezers is useful for plucking them out.

DIVISION: Divisions can be taken off existing clumps. Small portions from the outside edge of the clump make the best divisions and they should be carefully removed so as not to spoil the plant. Pot into a gritty spongy mix and keep in cool moist conditions until established.

DOODIA (Pukupuku or rasp ferns)

SPORES: Not difficult to raise from spores. Sow according to the technique described in chapter 2. Ripe sori can be found on plants at various times throughout the year.

DIVISION: *D. media* is the main species grown and is easily propagated by division. It has a short creeping rhizome and also produces stolons to form quite large patches or colonies. Once a stolon has formed a new crown with fronds, it can be removed and potted. Reduce the length of the fronds and keep in a moist shady situation until new growth commences.

DRACOPHYLLUM (Grass trees)

SEED: Not too difficult to raise from seed, which should be sown when fresh. Fresh seed sown in May germinated within 4 months. One grower recommends cool-moist stratification for 3 months before sowing. Germinate in cool conditions. The seed germinates readily, but seedlings grow slowly and can take a year or more before they are ready for pricking out. Because of their slow growth rate, the seedlings can quickly be smothered by liverwort, moss or pearlwort (*Sagina procumbens*). Sowing the seed according to the scree or bog techniques might help to prevent the growth of liverwort or pearlwort, but moss could still be quite a problem. Seed of most species ripens between February and May. It does not store well.

CUTTINGS: Most *Dracophyllum* species are difficult and seldom propagated from cuttings. *D. recurvum* is one which appears to be less difficult, but many other species have not even been tried. One grower found semi-hardwood cuttings made in April took 18 months to root. It is possible that soft semi-hardwood cuttings or softwood cuttings might be more successful. The time of year when cuttings are taken could also be a critical factor. Because of their very thick shoots, the larger species such as *D. traversii* and *D. latifolium* are likely to prove impossible to grow from cuttings and will probably always have to be raised from seed.

DRAPETES

Drapetes is also known as *Kelleria*.

SEED: Before sowing cool-moist stratify for 2–3 months. Germinate in cool to intermediate conditions.

The fruits are usually ripe from about late January until March. The seed stores well.

DIVISION: This is the most common method of propagation. Most species are easily divided, and with the cushion-forming species the divisions should only be taken off the outside of the cushion. All species produce numerous self-layered stems, particularly cultivated plants, which provides another easy method of propagation.

DROSERA (Sundew)

SEED: All species can be propagated from seed, which should be sown according to the bog technique described in chapter 2. The seed germinates best if kept in reasonably warm conditions. It should be sown when ripe, although it stores quite well and can be kept for sowing in the spring. Ripe seed can usually be collected from January to March. *D. peltata* ssp. *auriculata* generally flowers earlier and the seed may ripen as early as October or November.

CUTTINGS: Species such as *D. binata* can be propagated from root cuttings. Sections of root 12–25 mm long are laid on the surface of a peat/sand mixture and covered with about 10 mm of the same mix. They should be placed in a warm humid atmosphere and after about 2–3 weeks little buds should commence forming. They will increase in length until they break through the top of the mix (usually after about 5 weeks). When they are about 5 cm high they can be potted individually. Some exotic species of *Drosera* (notably *D. capensis*) can be grown from leaf cuttings and it is possible some of our native species could similarly be propagated. Species that form more than one crown can also be propagated by division.

DYSOXYLUM SPECTABILE (Kohe kohe)

SEED: Usually raised from seed, which must be sown when fresh. Germinate in intermediate to warm conditions. Seedlings are very susceptible to *Botrytis* and *Phytophthora*. Treat with a suitable fungicide before sowing and after germination. Seed usually ripens between May and August and does not store well.

CUTTINGS: *D. spectabile* is so easily raised from seed that it does not appear to be commonly propagated from cuttings. Firm semi-hardwood or hardwood cuttings would probably offer the best chance of success, particularly if they are given bottom heat. A. Maloy, in *Plants for Free*, suggests that root cuttings might also be successful.

ELAEOCARPUS (Hinau and pokaka)

SEED: The seeds are very slow and erratic to germinate and germination can take 3–5 years. One grower recommends cool-moist stratification for 3 months before sowing, but its effectiveness is not presently known. *Elaeocarpus* seeds have a very woody or stony outer covering (endocarp) and it is possible that hot-water treatment or a period of warm-moist strati-fication, or even both, could shorten the germination time. Ripe seed can usually be harvested from early autumn until early winter. It stores well.

CUTTINGS: Soft semi-hardwood cuttings taken in March or April are not too difficult to root providing the correct material is chosen. Cutting material should be young branchlets that have made reasonably vigorous growth, not the older twiggy stems that make only short annual growth, and are hard over most of their length. The best material is found on young nursery-grown or garden-grown plants and seldom on older plants. Cuttings would also be a way of propagating the adult forms of both species, thus eliminating the rather long-persistent juvenile phase. This would be particularly useful with *E. dentatus*, as it would be possible to produce plants that flower at a very early age rather than having to wait for anything up to 20 years. Hybrids such as *E.* 'Moana' can only be propagated from cuttings.

ELATOSTEMA RUGOSUM (Parataniwha)

SEED: Easily raised from seed and in suitable conditions self-sown seedlings appear within the vicinity of the parent plant. Germinate in cool to intermediate conditions. Sow when ripe or seed can be stored until convenient. The plant flowers over a very long period and ripe seed can be harvested from about September until May. The seed stores well.

DIVISION: *Elatostema* is very easily propagated by division. Because it has very soft growth the stems of divisions should be cut back quite severely to prevent excessive wilting.

ELINGAMITA JOHNSONII

SEED: Usually propagated from seed, which should be sown when fresh and kept in warm conditions for germination. Seed kept in cool conditions takes 2–3 years to germinate. The fruits are normally ripe in January or February. The seed does not store well.

CUTTINGS: Semi-hardwood cuttings will root but can be very slow. Treat with hormone. Cuttings taken in October and kept in cool conditions take 18 months to root. Rooting would probably be accelerated with the use of bottom heat.

ELYMUS TENUIS (Blue grass)

SEED: Sow when ripe. The seed can be lightly covered. Germinate in well-lit, cool to intermediate conditions, but provide shade from direct sunlight. Seed usually

ripens during January and February. It stores well.

DIVISION: Easily divided, but most growers probably prefer to propagate from seed.

EMBERGERIA GRANDIFOLIA

SEED: Not difficult to raise from seed, which should preferably be sown when fresh, as it has a limited storage life. Germinate in intermediate conditions. Slugs are very fond of the young seedlings. Ripe seed can usually be collected any time from December to January.

DIVISION: Older plants are easily propagated by division, which is best if carried out in early spring before the new foliage becomes too large.

ENTELEA ARBORESCENS (Whau)

SEED: Easily raised from seed. Fresh seed will usually germinate within 1–2 months. Warm conditions give quicker and easier germination. Depending on locality, seed is normally ripe between October and February. It stores well and remains viable for quite a long period.

CUTTINGS: *Entelea* can be propagated from softwood or soft semi-hardwood cuttings. They should be treated with hormone and are much easier to root in warm conditions. The leaves should be considerably reduced in size.

EPACRIS

SEED: The very fine seed should be sown according to either the scree technique or the bog technique as described in chapter 2. Sow as soon as the seed is ripe and keep under cool conditions, or cool-moist stratify for 2–3 months prior to sowing. Seed of *E. pauciflora* can usually be found at various times throughout the year. *E. alpina* has a more limited flowering period and its seed is usually ripe between January and March. The seedlings are very small and so mosses and liverworts can be a problem until they are large enough to prick out.

CUTTINGS: Both species can be propagated from semi-hardwood tip cuttings. Treat with hormone and root in cool conditions. Rooting can take 8–10 months. It would be worthwhile experimenting with removing the growing tips of the cuttings to find out whether it has any beneficial effect on rooting.

EPILOBIUM (Willow herb)

SEED: All species are easily raised from seed, which usually germinates freely. Germination takes about 2 weeks. The seed stores well and can be kept for quite a number of months. Seed of the various species ripens in summer and early autumn; some can be harvested over quite a long period, but others have a more limited season.

CUTTINGS: Species that have semi-woody stems (e.g., *E. wilsonii*) can be propagated from soft semi-hardwood cuttings. The time of year is immaterial as long as suitable cutting material is available. Rooting can take 1–2 months.

DIVISION: Creeping species such as *E. glabellum* and *E. macropus* are easily propagated by division.

ERYNGIUM VESICULOSUM (Southern sea holly)

SEED: Easily propagated from seed, which should be sown when fresh. The germination of older seed can be improved by soaking the seed in warm water for several hours before sowing. Germinate in cool to intermediate conditions. Seed usually ripens from about January to March. It stores reasonably well.

DIVISION: This is the easiest way to propagate this plant, which produces numerous stolons to form large patches. Each crown can be removed to produce a new plant.

EUPHORBIA GLAUCA (Waiuatua)

SEED: Not difficult to raise from seed, which should be sown when fresh. Germinate in intermediate conditions. The seedlings are prone to attack by *Botrytis*. Seed usually ripens between December and April. It does not store well.

DIVISION: This is the easiest way of propagating this plant. Clumps should be divided in the early spring before growth commences. Divisions should be put into a gritty mix or if the garden soil is suitable they can be directly planted out. It can also be propagated from softwood or soft semi-hardwood cuttings, if necessary.

EUPHRASIA (Eyebright)

Overseas species of *Euphrasia* are semi-parasitic on the roots of grasses and other plants, but it is not known whether any of the New Zealand species are similar. However, *E. cuneata* (tutumako) has been grown without being able to attach its roots to any other plant. There are both annual and perennial species.

SEED: Seed should be sown when ripe or dry stored until early spring before sowing. Germinate in cool to intermediate conditions. It would be a wise precaution to prick out the seedlings into pots containing one of the smaller native grasses. Alternatively, the seed can be sown around the grasses and the resultant seedlings allowed to grow in the containers. Seed of the various species ripens from December to March. It stores well.

FESTUCA

SEED: Easily raised from seed, which should be sown when fresh. The seeds are quite large and should be covered. Germinate in well-lit, cool to intermediate conditions and shade from direct sunlight. Fresh seed will germinate within 8–10 days. Depending on the species and locality, seed ripens between January and March. It stores well.

DIVISION: The species are easily propagated by division. Selected forms of *F. coxii* with good glaucous foliage should only be propagated in this way. The foliage of divisions should be cut back to about half of its length. New growth will soon appear.

FREYCINETIA BANKSII (Kie kie)

SEED: Propagated by seed, which should be sown when ripe. Germinate in warm conditions with a minimum temperature of 16°C. As an alternative, the first method of the bog technique, described in chapter 2, could be tried. The fruits of *Freycinetia* usually ripen between February and May. Nowadays it is not always easy to obtain ripe fruits because they are greedily eaten by rats and possums.

DIVISION: If young plants that have commenced branching are available it is possible to take rooted divisions or offsets from them. They should be potted using a well-drained spongy mix and kept in a warm humid atmosphere until they are established.

FUCHSIA

SEED: All native *Fuchsia* species can be propagated from seed, which should preferably be sown when ripe. Germinate in cool to intermediate conditions. Germination takes up to 4 weeks and there is usually a very good percentage. Seed of *F. excorticata* sown in March germinated within 23 days. *F. procumbens* seed that is cool-moist stratified for 4 months germinates in 16 days. One grower recommends cool-moist stratification for 1 month before sowing, but that hardly seems necessary in view of the fact that seed germinates so readily. Damping off can sometimes be a problem with newly germinated seedlings. *F. excorticata* commences flowering very early in the spring and, depending on locality, ripe fruits can be harvested between October and February. Birds very quickly eat them when ripe and it is sometimes necessary to harvest slightly green berries. *F. perscandens* has a shorter season and the berries are normally ripe between October and December. The berries of *F. procumbens* can usually be collected between January and May. On indoor specimens they may also be available at other times of the year. The seed stores well.

CUTTINGS: The two larger species (*F. excorticata* and *F. perscandens*) and the hybrid *F. x colensoi* are very easily propagated from softwood cuttings, which are available from late spring to mid-summer. They root within 2–4 weeks. All species can be propagated from semi-hardwood and hardwood cuttings, which when taken during September and October take up to 3–4 months to root.

DIVISION: Rooted divisions can be taken off small plants of *F. procumbens*. This is best done in early spring just as growth commences.

GAHNIA

SEED: Seed should be dry stored 5–6 months before sowing. Fresh seed takes 9–12 months to germinate. Seed of some species, dry stored for 5 months, germinated within 4–5 months. Other treatments to overcome dormancy such as soaking in hot water appear ineffective. *Gahnia* is very intolerant of root disturbance and the seedlings should be pricked out as soon as they are large enough to handle. The seed takes 9–12 months to ripen; for most species this is between about September and January, but ripe seeds remain on some plants for several months or more.

DIVISION: Gahnias appear to be very resentful of root disturbance and do not transplant or divide very well. The leaves of divisions very quickly roll inwards, even when shortened back to reduce transpiration, and the divisions have a marked reluctance to grow.

GAULTHERIA

SEED: Seed should be cool-moist stratified for 4–5 months before sowing. Germinate in cool to intermediate conditions. Seed of *G. antipoda* collected in April and stratified for 5 months took 10 weeks to germinate. Seed cool-moist stratified for 1–2 months and sown in June took 6–12 months to germinate. The seedlings are quite minute and rather slow-growing. One month after germination they can be no more than 2.5 mm across and have only two pairs of true leaves. The native species of *Gaultheria* have two kinds of fruits: those that have an enlarged and succulent calyx that looks like a berry (*G. antipoda* and *G. depressa*); the rest have dry capsules that split open to release the seeds. Fruits of most species ripen between January and April. In some North Island localities some species flower earlier and it is possible to collect ripe fruits as early as December. *G. oppositifolia* generally flowers between October and February so that ripe fruits can be collected from about December to July. Seed stores well.

CUTTINGS: Cuttings are not always easy to root and those that do often take several months. Soft semi-hardwood cuttings probably offer the best chance of rooting, which means taking cuttings much earlier than most people tend to do. I have mainly tried in the autumn when the wood has become quite hard, which is possibly the reason why most people fail.

DIVISION: *G. depressa* can be carefully divided. The divisions are self-layered stems and need a certain amount of care after removal. They should be potted into a spongy gritty mix and kept in a cool humid atmosphere until well established.

GENIOSTOMA RUPESTRE *var.* LIGUSTRIFOLIUM (Hangehange)

SEED: Mainly propagated from seed, which should be sown when fresh. Germinate in intermediate to warm conditions. Seed usually ripens between December and March and does not store well.

CUTTINGS: Not difficult to propagate from softwood cuttings taken in early summer or semi-hardwood cuttings taken from late summer to autumn. Treat with hormone and root in intermediate conditions.

GENTIANA (Gentian)

SEED: All species are propagated mainly from seed. There are two ways of treating the seed. (1) Sow when fresh and stand the pots outside in a cold shady place over winter. In early spring move the pots into a greenhouse, cold-frame or other warm situation to encourage germination. (2) Cool-moist stratify the seed for 5–6 months before sowing and then keep the seed in intermediate to warm conditions until germination occurs. I prefer to sow according to the scree technique described in chapter 2. Alternatively, it can be covered with a thin layer of the coarse siftings from sand. Germination can take up to 7 weeks or more, but sometimes less. It can be very erratic and it always pays to keep the pot of sown seed for some months after germination, as a second germination sometimes occurs. The best germination I have experienced was with a plant of *G. saxosa* growing by the edge of a gravel path. Every spring hundreds of seedlings germinated amongst the stones. Some species of *Gentiana* are annual (e.g. *G. spenceri*, *G. grisebachii* and *G. filipes*) and must be raised from seed each year. Others such as *G. corymbifera* are mono-carpic; that is, they grow for several seasons but die after flowering only once. They must be treated in a similar manner to the annual species. The truly perennial species, which continue growing after they flower, are also propagated from seed, but there is not the same necessity to continually propagate them. Some species will produce female-only plants, but most seedlings will be hermaphrodite. The various species flower over quite a long period and with some of the early-flowering annual species seed could be ripe in January. Many of the species flower in mid-season and their seed will ripen during late February or early April, but with late-flowering species such as *G. corymbifera* the seed may not be ripe until April or May. *Gentiana* seed stores quite well, but germination becomes more difficult and erratic with age.

GERANIUM

SEED: Seed is the easiest way to propagate the native species. It is also used for *G. traversii* 'Elegans', which comes quite true from seed. Sow when fresh or store for sowing in spring. Germinate in intermediate to warm conditions. Germination takes about 2–4 weeks and is probably improved if the fresh seed is held in dry storage for about 2 months before sowing. During spring and early summer self-sown seedlings usually appear around existing plants. Most species flower for several months and ripe seed can be collected over the duration of the flowering season. The seeds are ejected from their capsules by an explosive device and it is easier to collect them early in the morning when conditions are moister and the capsules less likely to explode. The seed stores well for quite long periods.

CUTTINGS: Cuttings can be taken just as growth commences in spring. When the shoots that grow from the crown are large enough to handle they should be carefully removed so as not to damage the parent plant. Treat with hormone and root in cool to intermediate conditions. G. 'Pink Spice' can only be propagated by this method.

DIVISION: *G. sessiliflorum* has a stout rootstock that is branched at the top and with a little care pieces can be removed with enough root on them to make them viable divisions. *G. microphyllum* can be similarly treated, and its creeping stems sometimes root into the soil and are easily removed. *G. traversii* is less accommodating and has few branches from its rootstock, but it is sometimes possible to divide it. Occasionally, its stems root in and produce offset plants.

GEUM

SEED: Fresh seed probably benefits from dry storage for about 2 months before being sown. Germination can occur within about 1 month. Cool-moist stratification does not appear to offer much benefit as seed that was cool-moist stratified for 2 months before sowing in June took 2–5 months to germinate, however one grower recommends cool-moist stratification for 1 month. Seed usually ripens between January and March. It stores well.

DIVISION: *G. parviflorum* and some forms of *G. leiospermum* have a central rootstock that branches at the top. Both can be divided if the crowns are carefully separated so that each has a portion of root. *G. uniflorum* and some forms of *G. leiospermum* have creeping rootstocks and can quite easily be divided. Pot divisions using a gritty spongy mix and keep in a cool moist place until well established.

GINGIDIA

SEED: If sown when fresh in March, seed will germinate within 2–3 months, whereas seed that was cool-moist stratified for 2 months and sown in June took up to 5 months to germinate. Soaking seed in warm water for several hours will help to improve germination. Germinate in cool to intermediate conditions. Seed of most species ripens between January and March. *G. montana* can flower as early as October so that ripe seed can be collected in December. The seed stores well.

DIVISION: *G. montana* and to a lesser extent *G. enysii* can produce several crowns from the central rootstock and if care is taken they can be divided. Each crown should have a portion of root. Cut back the foliage to reduce transpiration, pot into a gritty spongy mix and keep cool and shaded until well established.

GNAPHALIUM

SEED: The seed can be sown when fresh or cool-moist stratified for 2 months before sowing. Germinate in cool to intermediate conditions. Germination takes about 1 month. Seed usually ripens between January and March. It has a limited storage life.

DIVISION: Clumps are very easily divided at almost any time of the year.

GRISELINIA (Broadleaf)

SEED: Seed should be cool-moist stratified for at least 2 months before sowing. Results can be rather unreliable, as I have had seed that was stratified for 5 months and 4 months later had still not germinated. Seedlings can be susceptible to *Phytophthora* and at the first sign of attack a suitable fungicide should be applied. Depending on locality, the seed of both species ripens between February and May. It is not always easy to obtain seed of *G. lucida*. The seed does not store well.

CUTTINGS: *G. littoralis* and its cultivars are easily propagated from semi-hardwood cuttings taken mainly in autumn. Treat with hormone and root in cool to intermediate conditions. Rooting can take 2–3 months, but cuttings of *G. lucida* can sit for quite a long time without producing roots. One Auckland nursery has devised an unusual variation of the old 'split stem', or incision wounding, technique for difficult-to-root cuttings. The bases of a pair of cuttings are split and then interlocked together by inserting the split half of one through the split of the other. The interlocked cuttings are then planted as one. The leaves of both species should be reduced in size.

GUNNERA

SEED: Cool-moist stratify for 2 months before sowing. Germinate in cool conditions. Fruit of the various species ripens between January and February. The seed stores reasonably well.

DIVISION: This is the simplest and easiest method of propagation. The New Zealand species of *Gunnera* are stoloniferous and produce numerous crowns, each of which can be separated as a new plant. Some species produce male and female flowers on separate plants and it may be that only one sex is commonly cultivated. *G. hamiltonii* is a case in point. In this situation division is the only practical means of propagation.

HALOCARPUS

Formerly included in *Dacrydium*. All three species — *H. bidwillii*, *H. biformis* and *H. kirkii* — are in cultivation.

SEED: Seed, if obtainable, is the usual way of propagation. It should be cool-moist stratified for 3 months before sowing. Germinate in cool to intermediate conditions. Germination can be rather slow. Seeds usually ripen between March and April.

CUTTINGS: All three species can be propagated from cuttings and it is also possible to propagate the adult form this way, thus eliminating the juvenile phase. Semi-hardwood cuttings taken in January took 9 months to root. The bases of the cuttings should be wounded. When taking cutting material, select only shoots that have apical dominance (except for *H. bidwillii*) and will produce an erect plant.

HALORAGIS ERECTA (Toatoa)

SEED: Easily raised from seed, which should be sown when fresh. Germinate in intermediate conditions. Germination can occur within 1 month. Seed usually ripens between January and April. It stores well. *H. erecta* 'Wanganui Bronze' is best propagated from cuttings.

CUTTINGS: Soft semi-hardwood cuttings are easily rooted. Root in intermediate conditions. Rooting takes about 1–2 months. If the growing tips are liable to wilt because they are too soft, they should be removed.

HEBE

Numerous species and cultivars are grown. The species can easily be raised from seed but if they are growing close to other hebes there is always the possibility of hybridisation. With the exception of the 'whipcord' group, practically all are easily propagated from cuttings and, except when seedling-grown stock is required for special purposes, it is the normal means of propagation. Some 'whipcord' species are not too difficult from cuttings but others can be more difficult.

SEED: As a general rule, seed should be sown when fresh, although it does store well. It appears to make little difference whether the seed is sown immediately it is ripe, after 4 months of dry storage, or after being cool-moist stratified. Germination still occurs within 10 days to 1 month. Germination percentages are usually very good. In some districts downy mildew and damping off can completely destroy a batch of seedlings within a day or two. A suitable fungicide should be used to control it. Seedlings grow quite rapidly and need to be pricked out soon after germination. Because of the diversity of the genus, there is great variation in the flowering times of the various species and seed ripens throughout many months of the year. The majority of species ripen between January and April.

CUTTINGS: Hebes can be propagated from softwood, semi-hardwood and hardwood cuttings. By far the majority are propagated from semi-hardwood and short hardwood cuttings and, as long as suitable material can be obtained, the time of year is immaterial. Cuttings taken during mid-winter can take quite a long time to root and generally it is better to take them at more suitable times when rooting is quicker. Softwood cuttings are not always so satisfactory because of the difficulty of keeping them turgid. During the period February to April, soft semi-hardwood cuttings are the most satisfactory. Quite a number also propagate easily from long hardwood cuttings taken in early June and lined out in the open ground. Hormone treatment is not necessary, but if time is important it speeds up root initiation. Depending on the time of the year and the type of cutting, rooting can take 1–6 months.

GRAFTING: Standard hebes can be produced quite easily by grafting a desired variety or cultivar onto a cutting-grown rootstock of a suitable species. Because of its rapid and straight growth *H. barkeri* is very suitable as a rootstock. Side grafting appears to be the best method (refer to chapter 4).

HEDYCARYA ARBOREA (Pigeonwood)

SEED: Usually raised from seed, which can be sown when ripe or cool-moist stratified for 3 months before sowing. Seed sown when ripe in May and kept outdoors germinated the following October. Seed sown when fresh and given some protection germinates within 2 months. The seed usually ripens between March and May. It does not store well.

CUTTINGS: Semi-hardwood cuttings taken during March and April enable both male and female plants to be propagated, thus ensuring there is a pollinator for the female. Treat with hormone and root in intermediate conditions.

HELICHRYSUM

The main way of propagating *Helichrysum* is by cuttings. Seed is seldom used unless it is for some special reason. The hybrid *H.* 'Graeme Paterson' can only be propagated from cuttings. Some botanists now place the shrubby New Zealand species in the genus *Ozothamnus*.

SEED: The seed should be cool-moist stratified for 2 months before sowing. The scree technique is the most satisfactory way of sowing. Germinate in cool to intermediate conditions. Depending on the species germination can take 1–2 months. Seed of *H. intermedium*, *H. parvifolium*, *H. coralloides* and *H. plumeum* usually ripens between January and March. *H. aggregatum*, *H. bellidioides* and *H. filicaule* flower earlier and their seeds are usually ripe between December and February. The seed does not store well.

CUTTINGS: Semi-hardwood and hardwood cuttings, usually taken during March and April, are easy to root. Depending on the species rooting can take 4–6 months. Cuttings of *H. coralloides* taken at the end of October took 2 months to root. *H. coralloides*, *H. intermedium* and *H. parvifolium* are best grown from hardwood cuttings taken with a heel. The cuttings are simply torn off the branch. No attempt should be made to trim the heel, apart from just cutting off the ragged tail end, and the foliage is left on; any attempt to remove it will damage the stem too much. Treat with hormone before inserting into the rooting mix. Soft semi-hardwood cuttings of *H. bellidioides* and *H. filicaule* root quite easily, usually within only a few weeks. *H. aggregatum* is propagated from semi-hardwood or hardwood cuttings taken during March and April. Root in cool conditions.

HELIOHEBE

Until recently this genus was included in *Hebe*. The main species grown are *H. hulkeana*, *H. raoulii* and *H. lavaudiana*. Two hybrid cultivars, *H.* 'Fairfieldii' and *H.* 'Hagley Park', are also common and can only be propagated from cuttings.

SEED: Sow when fresh. Germinate in intermediate conditions. Germination should occur within 10–30 days. In some districts *Heliohebe* seedlings are even more prone to downy mildew and damping off than those of *Hebe*. At the first sign of trouble use a suitable fungicide. Slugs and snails are fond of the seedlings. Depending on the species, seed ripens between November and January and, as with *Hebe*, stores well.

CUTTINGS: Semi-hardwood and hardwood cuttings root quite easily if taken during February to April. Treat with hormone and root in cool to intermediate conditions. Cuttings taken from flowering plants in late October also root well, but it is not always easy to obtain suitable cutting wood at that time.

HERPOLIRION NOVAE-ZELANDIAE (Grass lily)

SEED: Seed should be cool-moist stratified for 2–3 months before sowing. Germinate in cool to intermediate conditions. Germination can be erratic. The seed ripens between January and March.

DIVISION: Easily increased by division and this is the usual way of propagation, particularly if it is desired to select forms with the best blue-coloured flowers.

HIBISCUS

SEED: Both species are easily raised from seed, which usually benefits from a period of dry storage before being sown. That is why seed held over winter and sown in the spring germinates better than seed sown as soon as ripe. Spring-sown seed will germinate within 2–4 weeks. Germinate in intermediate to warm conditions. Seed usually ripens during late summer and until growth ceases at the beginning of winter. In storage the seed remains viable for quite long periods. *H. trionum* is now considered to be doubtfully native.

HIEROCHLOE REDOLENS (Scented holy grass)

SEED: Can be raised from seed, but most easily propagated by division. Seed should be sown as for other grasses (refer to *Anamanthele*, *Chionochloa*, etc. for details). Seed ripens between January and February and stores well.

DIVISION: The creeping rhizomes are very easily divided. Reduce the foliage in length and pot the divisions to grow on for planting out.

HOHERIA (Lacebark, ribbonwood, houhere)

SEED: Easily raised from seed. Seed of *H. populnea*, *H. sexstylosa* and *H. angustifolia* should be sown when ripe. *H. glabrata* and *H. lyallii* should be cool-moist stratified for 2–3 months before sowing. Germinate in intermediate to warm conditions. Germination usually occurs within 3–4 weeks. Seed of *H. populnea* and *H. sexstylosa* generally ripens between April and July, *H. glabrata* and *H. lyallii* between January and March, and *H. angustifolia* between February and April. The seed stores well but should be checked for caterpillars, which eat it and can do a great deal of damage in storage. The eggs are often present on the seed when it is harvested. Harvesting the seed when the capsules are still greenish and before the eggs have been laid usually avoids this problem. Dusting stored seed with Derris Dust is an additional safeguard.

CUTTINGS: Firm semi-hardwood or hardwood cuttings can be taken at almost any time of the year that suitable material is available. Reduce the leaf area of cuttings to limit transpiration and, if necessary, also remove very soft growing tips. Treat with hormone and root in cool to intermediate conditions. Cuttings taken during the warmer months will root within 6–8 weeks and those taken during the colder months can take up to 8 months.

HOMALANTHUS POLYANDRUS

SEED: Generally propagated from seed. Sow as soon as ripe and germinate in warm conditions. Depending on the location seed can be available throughout the year. The seed stores well for short periods but does not keep for too long.

CUTTINGS: Semi-hardwood cuttings taken whenever suitable material is available can be rooted without too much difficulty. The leaves need to be cut back to reduce transpiration. Keep in warm conditions and treat with hormone.

HYPOLEPIS

SPORES: Sow according to the technique described in chapter 2. Ripe sori can be collected at various times during the growing season.

DIVISION: All species have creeping rhizomes and are easily propagated by division. Carefully dig up sections of rhizome that have several fronds and at least one growing tip. Cut off the fronds or reduce them to the 2–3 lower pinnae, and pot the rhizomes in a gritty spongy mix. Do not bury too deeply. Keep in a moist shady place until they are well established.

IPOMOEA CAIRICA

SEED: Seed should be scarified or given hot-water treatment before sowing. Needs to be kept in warm conditions for successful germination. Depending on the location seed ripens between January and April. It stores well.

DIVISION: Some growers propagate by division.

Rooted divisions are taken off the rootstock, potted and kept in warm conditions until established.

ISOLEPIS

Formerly included in the genus *Scirpus*. The species most likely to be grown is *I. cernua*. An exotic form of this species has long been grown in greenhouses, but the native form is quite distinct. The generic name is often misspelt 'Isolepsis'.

SEED: Seed can be sown when fresh, but it is probably better if given 2 months cool-moist stratification before sowing. Germinate in cool conditions. Germination is likely to be erratic. Seed is generally ripe between February and April.

DIVISION: This is the usual and by far the easiest way of propagation. Cut back the foliage, put in a pot and keep in lightly shaded conditions until established. Do not make the divisions too small.

ISOTOMA FLUVIATILIS

SEED: Sow when fresh. The seed is very small and should be left uncovered or have only the merest suggestion of a covering sifted over it. Germinate in intermediate conditions. Seed usually ripens between January and April. It stores well.

DIVISION: Generally propagated by division, which is the easiest way. Clumps or patches can be divided into numerous pieces, which quickly become established when potted.

IXERBA BREXIOIDES (Tawari)

SEED: Rather slow to germinate and should be given 3 months cool-moist stratification before sowing. Even then germination can take 2 months or more. Unstratified seed can take 7 months or longer to germinate. The seed usually ripens between December and February and does not store well.

CUTTINGS: Propagate from semi-hardwood cuttings, which can be very slow to root. Treat with hormone and root in cool to intermediate conditions. Cuttings taken in April took 11 months to root. The type of material and time of year could have a strong influence on the time taken for root initiation.

JOVELLANA

SEED: Not difficult to germinate and in some situations self-sown seedlings come up around the parent plant. The seed should be sown when fresh although, as with *Hebe*, germination could be quicker and more even after 1–2 months of dry storage. Seed of *J. sinclairii* ripens between about February and April. That of *J. repens* ripens between about March and April. It stores well.

CUTTINGS: *J. sinclairii* can also be propagated from softwood or soft semi-hardwood cuttings taken whenever suitable material is available. They should be kept in cool conditions for rooting. Depending on the time of the year and the kind of material used, rooting can take from about 6 weeks to 6 months. Cuttings taken during November give the best results. *J. repens* is much smaller and has very slender stems. It can be propagated from cuttings, but division would be more usual.

KNIGHTIA EXCELSA (Rewarewa)

SEED: Easily propagated from seed, which is usually sown when ripe. Needs warm conditions for good germination. Germination usually occurs within about 4–6 weeks. It is necessary to watch the young seedlings carefully for *Phytophthora*. Use a suitable fungicide if it appears.

The seed takes about 12 months to ripen, which is usually between October and December. Once the capsules ripen they open quickly, so it is necessary to be particularly watchful when ripening approaches. It is usually easy to harvest the seed from garden-grown trees, but it can be quite difficult with the taller forest trees. It stores quite well and, if necessary, can be stored for some months.

CUTTINGS: I have not heard of anybody propagating *K. excelsa* from cuttings, but there is no reason why it cannot be done. Many members of the Proteaceae can be propagated from cuttings, and cutting propagation of rewarewa would enable selected clones to be grown. Semi-hardwood cuttings taken during March and April should not be too difficult. Treat with hormone and root in intermediate conditions.

KUNZEA ERICOIDES (Kanuka)
(syn. *Leptospermum ericoides*)

SEED: Sow seed when fresh (germination occurs in about 1 month), or dry store for at least 2 months and then sow. With the latter, germination occurs within about 14 days. Germination is usually excellent. In some districts the seedlings can be susceptible to damping off. Use a suitable fungicide if it occurs. The seed ripens between March and May, but once the capsules commence to open it is quickly dispersed. Unopened capsules left in a warm situation usually open and shed their seeds within a day or two. The seed stores well.

CUTTINGS: Selected forms and cultivars are easily propagated from semi-hardwood cuttings taken during March and April. Treat with hormone and root in cool to intermediate conditions. Rooting should occur within 6–8 weeks.

LAGAROSTROBOS COLENSOI (Silver pine)
(syn. *Dacrydium colensoi*)

SEED: Propagate from seed, which should be cool-moist stratified for 1–2 months before sowing. Seeds usually ripen in April and May.

CUTTINGS: Can be propagated from semi-hardwood cuttings. Cuttings should be made from branchlets that have apical dominance so that they will grow upright and form a tree. Treat with hormone and root in cool to intermediate conditions.

LAGENIFERA

SEED: All species can be propagated from seed, which should be sown when fresh, preferably according to the scree technique described in chapter 2. Germinate in cool to intermediate conditions. The seed usually ripens between December and April, according to species and locality. It does not store well.

DIVISION: This is by far the easiest way to propagate *Lagenifera* species. Either small clumps or single rosettes can be divided off. Pot and keep in a cool moist situation until established.

LASTREOPSIS

SPORES: Sow according to the technique described in chapter 2. Ripe sori of the various species can usually be collected from about December until March, although they might also be available earlier in the season. *L. glabella*, in particular, is very easily raised from spores. The species with tufted rhizomes can only be propagated from spores. Those with creeping rhizomes can also be propagated by division.

DIVISION: Both *L. hispida* and *L. microsora* can be propagated from divisions. Short pieces of rhizome bearing a terminal growth and one or two fronds should be removed from the parent plant. Cut back the fronds so that only 2–3 pairs of the lower pinnae remain, pot into a gritty spongy mix and keep in a cool shady place until new growth commences. Do not bury the rhizomes too deeply.

LAURELIA NOVAE-ZELANDIAE (Pukatea)

SEED: Sow when fresh and keep in cool conditions for germination. The seed usually ripens between October and January. It does not store well for any length of time.

CUTTINGS: It is probable that pukatea can be propagated from cuttings, but I have not heard of anybody who has done so.

LEPIDOTHAMNUS

Formerly in the genus *Dacrydium*. There are two

species (*L. laxifolius* and *L. intermedius*), both of which are cultivated.

SEED: Seed should be cool-moist stratified for 1–2 months before sowing. Germinate in cool conditions. Seed usually ripens in April and May.

CUTTINGS: Propagate from semi-hardwood cuttings. Treat with hormone and root in cool conditions. Semi-hardwood cuttings taken in May took 10 months to root.

LEPTINELLA
(syn. *Cotula*)

SEED: For lowland species the seed should be sown when ripe, but for alpine species such as *L. pyrethrifolia*, *L. atrata* and *L.dendyi* it should be cool-moist stratified for 2 months before sowing. The seed apparently does not store well. The flowering times of the various species are rather diverse, but most probably ripen their seeds between December and March.

DIVISION: The principal way of propagating *Leptinella* species is by division and, with one or two exceptions, it is simple and easy. Most are mat-forming plants and it is only necessary to divide pieces off the outside edges of the mat. They re-establish very easily. *L. atrata* and *L. dendyi* require a little more care with the dividing, but they cannot be regarded as being exceptionally difficult. *L. atrata* ssp. *luteola* is easier than *L. atrata*, and really not much more difficult than the commoner mat-forming species. Species used for the surfacing of bowling greens are usually propagated by chopping the rhizomes into small pieces and sowing them as for seed. Although not a common practice, species such as *L. pyrethrifolia* can be propagated from cuttings.

LEPTOCARPUS SIMILIS (Oioi, jointed rush)

SEED: Sow when fresh. Germinate in cool conditions. Germination can take quite some time and can be erratic. Seed usually ripens between December and March.

DIVISION: This is the easiest and usual way of propagating this plant. Reasonably large divisions are better than those that are too small; pieces about the size of a clenched fist are the best.

LEPTOLEPIA NOVAE-ZELANDIAE

SPORES: Sow according to the technique described in chapter 2. Ripe sori can generally be collected between December and March.

DIVISION: Remove short lengths of rhizome, preferably having a growing tip and 2 or 3 fronds. Cut off the fronds leaving only their stalks or the

2–3 lower pinnae and pot into a gritty spongy mix. Keep in a cool shady place until new growth appears.

LEPTOPTERIS (Crepe fern and Prince of Wales feathers)

SPORES: Sow according to the technique described in chapter 2. *L. hymenophylloides*, in particular, is quite easy to propagate and when it is grown in an indoor fernery sporelings appear with great freedom. Ripe sori of both species can be obtained at various times throughout the growing season.

LEPTOSPERMUM SCOPARIUM (Manuka)

SEED: Sow when fresh. Germinate in intermediate conditions. Germination will occur within 10 days or so. The seed stores well and seed dry stored for 5 months still germinated within about 10 days. Usually there is a very good germination percentage. According to district, altitude and other factors, seed capsules ripen between September and June, and throughout the year it is usually possible to collect unopened capsules of the previous year's flowering. In some areas all capsules open fairly soon after ripening. The seed stores well. The typical form can be propagated from seed or cuttings, but selected forms and cultivars are propagated from cuttings only.

CUTTINGS: Firm semi-hardwood or hardwood cuttings taken during March to May give the best results. Traditionally, most people take fairly short cuttings 5–10 cm long, but there is an advantage in taking cuttings up to 15 or 20 cm long. Fairly vigorous shoots make the best long cuttings. The longer cuttings are no more difficult to root and a larger plant is obtained more quickly. Treat with hormone and root in intermediate conditions. Wounding the cuttings also assists with rooting.

LEUCOGENES (New Zealand edelweiss)

SEED: Sow as soon as ripe and leave over winter in cool conditions, or cool-moist stratify for 2–3 months before sowing. Sow according to the scree technique described in chapter 2. Germinate in cool conditions. The seed probably has a short viability period and, in common with many members of the daisy family, often produces many infertile seeds. Seed usually ripens between February and April.

CUTTINGS: Semi-hardwood cuttings taken during March and April give the best results. Treat with hormone and root in cool conditions. Rooting takes about 2 months.

DIVISION: Larger clumps of *Leucogenes* species can be propagated by division. Divisions should be potted into a gritty free-draining mix and kept in cool lightly shaded conditions until established.

LIBERTIA (New Zealand iris)

SEED: Sow when fresh. Germinate in cool to intermediate conditions. Germination takes 5–6 months. Dry storing the seed at various temperatures and cool-moist stratification appear to make little difference to the germination time. Hot-water treatment is recommended as a way of hastening germination by one grower. There is usually an excellent germination percentage. Seed usually ripens between January and May, but both *L. ixioides* and *L. peregrinans* can flower intermittently so that it is sometimes possible to harvest ripe seed at various times throughout the year. In addition, the ripe seed capsules of *L. ixioides* sometimes remain on the plant for quite some time. The seed stores well.

DIVISION: All species divide easily and it is the quickest way of producing new plants. Clumps should be lifted and broken up in the early spring before growth commences. Each fan will produce a new plant. Cut back the foliage by at least half and trim back the roots to about 5–7 cm long. Replant the fans directly into the open ground or put into containers. If a larger plant is required plant several fans together. *L. pulchella* has more specialised requirements and is usually grown in containers only.

LIBOCEDRUS (New Zealand cedar)

SEED: This is usually the only method of propagation. Sow when fresh or cool-moist stratify for 2 months before sowing. Germinate in cool to intermediate conditions. The seed does not store well.

CUTTINGS: Propagate from semi-hardwood cuttings taken during March and April, but they can be difficult to root. One grower has found that cuttings callus well but take 2 years to form roots. It is possible that soft, rather than firm, semi-hardwood cuttings might be more successful. Wounding and treating batches of cuttings with each of the full range of hormones could also produce quicker results. It would also pay to experiment with taking cuttings at other times of the year, such as July or early November.

LINUM MONOGYNUM (Rauhuia)

SEED: Easily raised from seed, which should be sown when fresh. Germinate in intermediate conditions. Germination usually occurs within about 2 months or less. Self-sown seedlings often appear around parent plants. Seed usually ripens between December and February, although because of the plant's long-flowering habit it can often be harvested outside of those months. It stores well.

CUTTINGS: Softwood or soft semi-hardwood cuttings taken during February and March root easily. According to A. Maloy in *Plants for Free*, it can also be propagated from root cuttings.

LITSEA CALICARIS (Mangeao)

SEED: Sow when fresh or cool-moist stratify for 2 months before sowing. Germinate in cool to intermediate conditions. The fruits ripen during October and November.

CUTTINGS: Mangeao is not usually propagated from cuttings but it can be done. The tree is dioecious (has male and female flowers on separate trees) and cuttings would be the only way to be certain of obtaining plants of both sexes. Semi-hardwood cuttings taken in May took 10 months to root. Possibly softwood or soft semi-hardwood cuttings might give better results. Cuttings of more juvenile material should also be tried.

LOBELIA

SEED: The seed of *L. anceps* can be sown when fresh, but that of the two alpine species (*L. linnaeoides* and *L. roughii*) should be either dry stored and sown in spring or cool-moist stratified for 2–3 months before sowing. The seed is very fine and needs little or no covering when sown. Sow the two alpine species according to the scree method described in chapter 2. Germinate in cool to intermediate conditions. Seed of *L. anceps* ripens between November and April, that of *L. linnaeoides* between January and April, and *L. roughii* between December and April. It stores well.

DIVISION: *L. linnaeoides* is very easily propagated by dividing the creeping mats into suitable pieces. *L. roughii* can be divided providing great care is taken, but is better propagated from seed.

LOPHOMYRTUS

SEED: Cool-moist stratify for 2–3 months before sowing. Seed of *L. obcordata* stratified for 3 months and sown in late September germinated within 16 days. A batch of seed stratified for 5 months and sown at the same time took 36 days to germinate. Germinate in cool to intermediate conditions. Seedlings are prone to damping off. Treat with a suitable fungicide if it appears. Fruits usually ripen from March to May and the seed stores well.

CUTTINGS: Semi-hardwood and hardwood cuttings taken during March and April give good results. Treat with hormone and root in cool to intermediate conditions. Cultivars and the hybrid *L. x ralphii* can only be propagated from cuttings.

LOXSOMA CUNNINGHAMII

SPORES: Sow according to the technique described in chapter 2. Ripe sori can be collected at various times throughout the growing season.

DIVISION: Not difficult to propagate by division of the rather stout rhizome. Pieces of rhizome having several fronds and a terminal growth should be removed and potted into a gritty spongy mix. Reduce the size of the fronds to the 2–3 lower pinnae. Keep in a cool humid atmosphere until new growth appears and the division is well established. Do not bury the rhizome too deeply.

LUZULA (Wood rush)

SEED: Sow when fresh or cool-moist stratify for 2 months before sowing. Germinate in cool conditions. Seed germinates easily. The various species usually ripen their seeds between about December and March. The seed stores well.

DIVISION: Easily propagated by division. It is not necessary to cut back the foliage of the smaller-leaved species, but for those with larger leaves they should be reduced by about half. Pot the divisions and keep lightly shaded until established.

LUZURIAGA PARVIFLORA (Forest snowberry)

SEED: Sow when fresh or cool-moist stratify for 2–3 months before sowing. Seed stratified for 2 months took over 1 year to germinate. The seed-sowing mix needs to be spongy and well-drained so that it does not compact and become too wet. Germinate in cool conditions. Fruit mainly ripens between January and April, but ripe fruits can often be found throughout the year.

DIVISION: Well-grown plants can be divided. The creeping stems should be carefully cut apart and the divisions potted into a spongy humus-rich mix. Keep in a cool shady place until established.

MACHAERINA SINCLAIRII (Pepepe, toetoe tuhara)

SEED: Sow when fresh or cool-moist stratify for 2 months before sowing. Germinate in cool to intermediate conditions. Seed usually ripens between December and February. It stores well.

DIVISION: Easily propagated by division, which should be carried out in early spring just as growth commences. Reduce the length of the leaves on each fan by about half or more and shorten the roots to about 10–15 cm long. Replant directly into the open ground or pot until established before planting out.

MACROPIPER EXCELSUM (Kawakawa, pepper tree)

SEED: Sow when fresh. Depending on whether the seed is given bottom heat or kept in cool conditions,

germination takes 4–6 weeks or up to 5 months. *Phytophthora* can be a problem in some parts of the country. The first visible symptoms show on the leaves. Treat with a suitable fungicide. In some localities ripe fruits are found on plants throughout the year, but in many areas the main fruiting period appears to be from January to about March. The seed stores well.

CUTTINGS: Cultivars and selected clones are propagated from cuttings. Soft semi-hardwood cuttings taken whenever suitable material is available root quite easily. Treat with hormone and bottom heat will hasten rooting. Cuttings kept in cool conditions can take 3–6 months to root.

MARATTIA SALICINA (Para, king fern)

SPORES: Sow according to the technique described in chapter 2. Ripe sori can be collected at various times throughout the growing season. Not usually raised from spores.

AURICLES: These are the swollen basal portions of the frond stalks (stipites), which adhere to the large rootstock after the frond dies. Carefully remove some of the lowest ones from an older plant and partially bury in a suitable mix. Refer to chapter 4 for further details. Basal sprouts appear on some plants and they can also be taken off as divisions.

MAZUS

SEED: Sow when ripe or dry store for 2–3 months before sowing. Germinate in intermediate conditions. Germination usually occurs within about 4 weeks or so. The seed capsules of *M. radicans* usually ripen between April and June. They often turn bright reddish when ripe. Those of *M. pumilio* (now regarded as a different species) ripen between January and April. The seed stores well.

DIVISION: Very easily propagated by division. Take the divisions from the outside edges of the mat. Pot and keep shaded until they become established.

MELICOPE

SEED: The seed germinates easily and should be sown when fresh. Germinate in cool to intermediate conditions. Seed of *M. ternata* ripens between November and February and that of *M. simplex* between March and April. It stores well.

CUTTINGS: Semi-hardwood cuttings should be taken during March and April. Treat with hormone and root in cool to intermediate conditions. Cuttings taken during October took 7 months to root. Selected clones and the hybrid *M.* x *mantellii* should be propagated from cuttings.

MELICYTUS

SEED: Sow when fresh or cool-moist stratify for 4–5 months before sowing. Germinate in cool or intermediate conditions. Fresh seed of *M. ramiflorus* sown in March germinated within 2 months, whereas seed sown after stratification for 2 months took 6 months to germinate. Seed of *M. ramiflorus* stratified for 5 months and sown in September germinated in just over 2 months. Seed of *M. alpinus* leached beforehand and given the same period of stratification had not germinated over 4 months later. Seed of most species ripens between February and April with *M. ramiflorus* usually ripening from January to May and *M. micranthus* is often ripe at various times of the year. The seed stores well.

CUTTINGS: Semi-hardwood cuttings taken from February to April give the best results. Treat with hormone and root in cool to intermediate conditions. Cuttings of all species except *M. alpinus* and *M. crassifolius* root fairly easily. The two latter species have thick twiggy shoots and are more difficult. Cuttings are used for selected clones and to obtain known plants of both the male and female.

MENTHA CUNNINGHAMII (Hioi, native peppermint)

SEED: Sow when fresh or dry store and sow in spring. The latter probably gives quicker and more even germination. Germinate in intermediate conditions. Seed ripens between December and February and stores well.

DIVISION: Easily divided at almost any time during the growing season. Reduce the length of the stems on divisions so that they recover more quickly. Also easily propagated from softwood cuttings.

MERYTA SINCLAIRII (Puka)

SEED: Sow when fresh and germinate in warm conditions. Seed can ripen between about December and June. It does not store well. The variegated cultivars are propagated either from cuttings or by grafting.

CUTTINGS: Semi-hardwood cuttings are not too difficult to root. Cuttings should be made from branchlets that are not too thick. The leaves need to be reduced in size or they can be rolled to make the cuttings easier to insert. They can be taken any time that suitable material is available. Treat with hormone and root in intermediate conditions.

GRAFTING: If it is not possible to obtain suitable cutting material, slightly thicker stems of the variegated cultivars can be grafted onto seedling rootstocks. See chapter 4 for details.

METROSIDEROS (Rata and pohutukawa)

SEED: With the exception of *M. umbellata*, seed of all species should be sown when fresh or it can be dry stored for 3 months before sowing. Keep in warm conditions for germination. A period of dry storage probably gives quicker and more even germination. Seed sown when fresh took 2 months to germinate. *M. umbellata* seed should be given 6 months cool-moist stratification before sowing. Germinate in intermediate temperature conditions. The seed of all species is very fine and should be left uncovered on the surface or given the merest suggestion of a covering. Allow the seedlings to grow 3–4 pairs of true leaves before pricking out. If they are pricked out when too small it can check their growth. Seed of *M. excelsa*, *M. robusta* and most climbing species usually ripens during July and August, that of *M. fulgens* about November and December and *M. carminea* from about December to March. Seed of *M. umbellata* takes over a year to mature and usually ripens between February and April. The seed stores well.

CUTTINGS: Not all *Metrosideros* species are easy to propagate from cuttings and *M. excelsa*, *M. robusta* and *M. umbellata* can be rather difficult. Strangely, *M. kermadecensis* is easier from cuttings than its close relative *M. excelsa*. Semi-hardwood cuttings taken at all times of the year have a low strike rate and take up to 9 months or more to root. One grower recommends taking softwood cuttings of *M. umbellata* in October. Most climbing species are not too difficult, although at times some can take a long time to root. Treat with hormone and root in cool to intermediate conditions.

Cuttings probably should be soft semi-hardwood rather than firm semi-hardwood and it could be worthwhile experimenting with various degrees of softwood cuttings at differing times of the year. Cuttings taken from adult forms of climbing species produce small and shrubby plants that do not retain their climbing habit. This has been exploited on a commercial scale with *M. carminea*; the cultivars 'Carousel' and 'Ferris Wheel' are both selected adult forms. To propagate the climbing species as climbers, it is necessary to use material from plants or parts of the plant that have not yet assumed the adult form.

GRAFTING: Because of the difficulty of rooting cuttings of *M. excelsa* some growers have resorted to grafting selected clones and cultivars. Side grafting is the best technique to use. Refer to chapter 4 for further details.

MICROLAENA

SEED: Sow when ripe or dry store for 2 months before sowing. Leave the sown seed uncovered or give just the merest suggestion of a covering. Germinate in cool to intermediate, well-lit conditions. Shade only from direct sunlight. The seed stores well and usually ripens between January and February.

DIVISION: Easily propagated by division. The foliage of divisions should be cut back to about half of its length. Pot divisions and keep in a cool shady place until new growth commences.

MIMULUS REPENS

SEED: Sow when fresh or dry store for 2 months before sowing. Germinate in cool conditions. Seed usually ripens between January and March. It stores well.

DIVISION: Easily propagated by division. Small rooted pieces taken off the parent plant and potted will soon form new plants suitable for planting out. Individual stems root very easily and can also be taken as cuttings.

MUEHLENBECKIA

SEED: Not difficult to raise from seed, which should be cool-moist stratified for 2 months before sowing. Germinate in intermediate conditions. Germination should occur within about 1 month. Seed of the various species usually ripens between February and April. It stores well.

CUTTINGS: All species can be propagated from semi-hardwood or hardwood cuttings taken between April and June. *M. astonii* is better if taken in June after it has lost its leaves.

DIVISION: *M. axillaris* propagates very easily by division. Rooted pieces taken from the parent plant and potted soon re-establish to make good plants. *M. ephedroides* can similarly be propagated.

MYOPORUM

SEED: Easily raised from seed, which is usually sown when fresh. One grower recommends scarifying the seed before sowing. Germinate in intermediate conditions. Seed usually ripens between February and April. It stores well.

CUTTINGS: Can be propagated from softwood and soft semi-hardwood cuttings, which can be taken whenever suitable material is available. Treat with hormone and root in intermediate conditions. Depending on the time of the year, rooting can take from 2–10 months.

MYOSOTIDIUM HORTENSIA (Chatham Island forget-me-not)

SEED: Seed can be sown when fresh, but germination is erratic and often does not occur until spring. If given cool-moist stratification for 1 month before sowing a more even germination occurs. The various colour forms of *Myosotidium* come true from seed, as long as they have not been cross-pollinated with each other. Germinate in cool conditions. Seed usually ripens in December and January. It will keep in dry storage for up to 12 months or more.

DIVISION: Older plants can be divided quite easily. This should be carried out in early spring before growth commences. Lift the plants so as to retain as much root as possible and cut the rhizomes into pieces, making sure that each has a crown or growing tip. Remove all of the large old foliage before replanting or potting. Renovate the soil, adding plenty of humus, and replant with the rhizomes partly buried.

MYOSOTIS (Forget-me-not)

SEED: Sow when fresh or dry store for 2 months before sowing. The latter gives a more even germination. I have found that the best way to sow the seed is by the scree technique as described in chapter 2. Just scatter the seeds among the surface layer of stone chips and they come up very easily. Germinate in cool conditions. Germination usually occurs within about 4–8 weeks. In some districts the newly germinated seedlings can be attacked by mildew and damping off. If that is a regular problem use a suitable fungicide as a preventive. According to species, the seed ripens between November and April. Seed of *M. uniflora* and *M. pulvinaris* is usually sunk into the cushions and it is often necessary to use a pair of tweezers to collect it. *Myosotis* seed keeps well in storage. All of the native species propagate easily from seed, but hybrids must be propagated vegetatively.

DIVISION: The majority of *Myosotis* species and hybrids propagate easily by division. Some can be divided at almost any time of the year, but species with large leaves should preferably be divided in spring just as growth commences. *M. pulvinaris* does not divide easily but *M. uniflora* does. One or two species produce stolons and it is a very simple task to remove the rooted stolons and transplant them.

CUTTINGS: Species such as *M. eximia*, which has woody stems, can also be propagated from soft semi-hardwood cuttings taken from January to March. Root in cool conditions. Most root quite easily.

MYRSINE

SEED: Cool-moist stratifyfor 2–3 months before

sowing. Germinate in cool to intermediate conditions. Germination is slow and can take from 2 to perhaps 18 months. Seed of *M. australis* and *M. salicina* takes about 12 months to ripen. The former ripens in autumn and the latter from spring to late summer. Both *M. divaricata* and *M. nummularia* ripen between March and May.

CUTTINGS: All species and the cultivar of *M. australis* can be propagated from semi-hardwood or hardwood cuttings. Root in cool to intermediate conditions. The best results are from cuttings taken in April, and rooting can take up to 12 months with cuttings of *M. chathamica* taking up to 3 years. *M. salicina* is another species that takes a long time to root. Hardwood cuttings of *M. divaricata* taken in April took about 6 months to root. It is also possible to take rooted divisions off small plants of *M. nummularia*.

NEOMYRTUS PEDUNCULATA

SEED: Cool-moist stratify for 2–3 months before sowing. Germinate in cool to intermediate conditions. Seedlings can be prone to damping off. Treat with a suitable fungicide if it appears. Seeds usually ripen from March to May. The seed stores well.

CUTTINGS: Semi-hardwood and hardwood cuttings taken during March and April give good results. Treat with hormone and root in intermediate conditions.

NEOPAXIA AUSTRALASICA

SEED: Cool-moist stratify for 1–2 months before sowing. Germinate in intermediate conditions. Seed usually ripens during February and March and stores well.

DIVISION: Very easily propagated by division of the creeping stems. Pot divisions until established.

NEPHROLEPIS SPECIES (Ladder fern)

This fern was formerly mistakenly identified as *N. cordifolia*, a tropical species commonly cultivated in New Zealand. The generic name is often misspelt 'Nephrolepsis'.

SPORES: Sow according to the technique described in chapter 2. Ripe sori can be collected at various times throughout the year.

DIVISION: The stoloniferous nature of this fern lends itself to propagation by division. Simply wait until the new crown at the tip of the stolon has produced roots, sever it from the parent, cut back the fronds by about two-thirds and put it into a pot. Keep it in a humid atmosphere until new growth commences.

NERTERA

SEED: Cool-moist stratify the seed for 2 months before sowing. The seed germinates best in intermediate conditions. Seed of the various species usually ripens between January and May. It stores well.

DIVISION: Being creeping plants that form matted patches, the species of *Nertera* propagate very easily by division. Divisions should be potted and kept in a shady place until established.

NESTEGIS (Maire)

SEED: Cool-moist stratify for 2–3 months and then germinate in a warm temperature. For sowing fresh seed, cut the end off the endocarp (the stony covering of the seed), taking care not to damage the embryo inside, and then sow immediately. The seeds often have a low germination percentage. Germination can be slow and erratic. The seed of the various species usually ripens between January and April.

CUTTINGS: Semi-hardwood cuttings from vigorous stems should be taken from about December to February. Bottom heat helps to induce rooting. Treat with hormone.

NOTHOFAGUS (Southern beeches)

SEED: Cool-moist stratify for 2–3 months before sowing. Germinate in intermediate conditions. Seed usually ripens between March and April. For several years *Nothofagus* sets few viable seeds and there is then a season when large quantities of viable seeds are set. The seed soon loses its viability if kept in dry storage.

CUTTINGS: *Nothofagus* can be propagated from cuttings but they are quite difficult. From the current state of knowledge, semi-hardwood cuttings appear to be the best. Tip cuttings 3–5 cm long taken with a heel and collected from young trees in October appear to give the best results. Treat with 0.3% or 0.5% IBA and root in cool conditions. It is possible that experimentation with softwood cuttings taken in November or December and given various treatments could give greater success. There are three cultivars, only one of which (*N. fusca* 'Bert Newman') has been regularly propagated. A weeping form of *N. menziesii* (not yet in cultvation) and a dwarf form of *N. solandri* have yet to be successfully propagated. There is also the possibility that these cultivars could be grafted.

NOTOSPARTIUM (Pink broom)

SEED: The seed should be given hot-water treatment (90°C and soaked for 24 hours) before sowing. Germinate in intermediate conditions. Germination will occur within about 10 days. Seed cool-moist stratified for 2 months germinates within 3–4 weeks. Seed usually ripens in February and March and stores well.

CUTTINGS: Semi-hardwood or hardwood cuttings (preferably with heels) taken during March and April are not too difficult to root. Treat with hormone and root in cool to intermediate conditions.

NOTOTHLASPI

SEED: Cool-moist stratify for 2–3 months before sowing. Keep in intermediate temperatures for germination which usually occurs in the spring. Refer to the article by Grant Bawden (*Bull. N.Z. Alpine Gard. Soc.* No. 62, p. 27–28, June 1994) for further details of growing *N. rosulatum* from seed. *N. australe* would probably require similar treatment. Seed ripens form January to March and stores well.

OLEARIA

SEED: Some growers recommend cool-moist stratification for 1 month, but there appears to be little difference when the seed is sown when fresh, dry stored for 2–3 months or stratified. Seed of *O. avicenniifolia* dry stored for 4 months and sown in late September germinated within 15–18 days; seed stratified for 4 months and sown at the same time germinated within 8 days. Sow according to the scree technique described in chapter 2 or, if sown in the usual manner, barely cover the seed. Germinate at medium temperatures. There is a great variability in the flowering times of *Olearia* species and a consequent similar variation in the ripening times for seed. The seed of early-flowering species such as *O. fragrantissma* can be expected to ripen about November, whereas with late-flowering species such as *O. avicenniifolia* and *O. paniculata* the seed can ripen as late as July. With the majority of species the seed ripens during the January to March period. The viability varies from species to species as well as from season to season. Seed from garden-grown plants sometimes has better viability than that collected from wild plants. The seed of most species can be stored for at least 6 months without losing too much viability.

CUTTINGS: Cuttings are the commonest means of propagation. Selected clones, hybrids and cultivars can only be propagated from cuttings. Most species are easily propagated from firm semi-hardwood or hardwood cuttings taken from March to May. Cuttings can be taken at other times of the year, but rooting can take quite a bit longer. As well as short hardwood cuttings, some of the commoner olearias are quite easily grown from long hardwood cuttings taken in early June and lined out in the open ground. Treat cuttings with hormone. The provenance can

make a difference with the ease of rooting some species. For example, South Island plants of *O. hectorii* are not difficult to propagate, but cuttings from central North Island populations of this species are much more so. *O. fragrantissima* is very difficult from cuttings and few propagators have mastered it. *O. chathamica* and *O. semidentata* are very prone to attack by *Phytophthora* and with these species, more or less continuous propagation is necessary to maintain a supply of young plants as replacements.

ORCHIDS

SEED: Many of the terrestrial orchids are not too difficult to raise from seed. Scatter the seeds over the surface of the potting mix in which the particular species is growing. A mulch over the pot is beneficial. Seedlings should appear the following spring. The epiphytic species (e.g., *Dendrobium* and *Earina*) require a slightly different technique. For further details regarding both kinds refer to chapter 2.

DIVISION: The epiphytic and evergreen terrestrial species are easily propagated by removal of offsets. Deciduous terrestrial species are tuberous and easily split up while dormant.

OURISIA

SEED: Cool-moist stratify for 1–2 months before sowing. The seed is probably best if sown according to the scree technique described in chapter 2. Germinate in cool to intermediate conditions. Germination usually takes 1–2 months. Seed usually ripens between January and April. It does not store well.

DIVISION: All species divide easily. Pot divisions into a gritty spongy mix and keep in a cool shady place until established. *Phytophthora* or *Rhizoctonia* can sometimes be a problem and at the first sign of trouble use a suitable fungicide.

OXALIS MAGELLANICA

SEED: Dry store for 1–2 months before sowing. Germinate in cool conditions. Seed ripens from January to March and stores well.

DIVISION: This is the usual way of propagating this species and the double-flowered cultivar can only be propagated by this method. Divisions are quick to establish if kept in a cool situation.

PACHYSTEGIA (Marlborough rock daisy)

SEED: All species and selected clones are easily raised from seed. Sow when fresh or dry store for 1 month before sowing. The seed can be sown as normal, but I prefer the scree technique. Where plants grow alongside gravel pathways the seed often germinates very freely in the gravel. Germination usually takes 7–10 days. Some growers recommend cool-moist stratification for 1 month before sowing. Keep seedlings on the dry side to prevent *Phytophthora* or damping off. Slugs and snails are very fond of the seedlings. With the exception of *P. minor*, seed usually ripens between February and April. *P. minor* usually flowers 2–3 weeks later than the other species and its seed often ripens between April and May. Seed stores reasonably well for periods of up to about 6 months. The different species and clones will hybridise, so if collecting seed for propagation it should be from plants that do not have the opportunity to hybridise or cross. This particularly applies to *P. rufa* and already hybrids between this and *P. insignis* are in the nursery trade under the name of *P. rufa*.

CUTTINGS: Firm semi-hardwood or hardwood cuttings of *P. minor* are relatively easy to root, but the other species are rather more difficult. Thinner shoots are easier to strike than the very thick ones. Cuttings should be taken between March and April. Treat with hormone and root in cool to intermediate conditions. Rooting can take up to 6 months.

PAESIA SCABERULA (Lace fern)

SPORES: Sow according to the technique described in chapter 2. Ripe sori usually occur on the plant throughout much of the growing season.

DIVISION: Can be propagated by division of its creeping rhizomes, but not quite as easily as some other species. The divisions should be of generous size and not too deeply buried in a gritty spongy mix. Reduce the length of the fronds to the 2–3 lower pairs of pinnae and keep in a shady place until new growth appears.

PARAHEBE

SEED: Easily raised from seed, which can be sown when fresh or dry stored for 1–2 months before sowing. The latter possibly gives more even germination. Germination usually occurs within 15–30 days but, depending on the time of year and conditions, could take up to 2 months. As with *Hebe*, damping off of the young seedlings can be a problem. If it appears use a suitable fungicide. Seed of most species ripens between January and May. Some species such as *P. catarractae* and *P. lyallii* flower over several months and it is often possible to harvest ripe seed over a very long period. It stores well.

CUTTINGS: Semi-hardwood cuttings taken during March to April give the best results, although they can be successfully taken at other times. Treat with hormone and root in cool to intermediate conditions.

Rooting occurs in about 2–3 months. Some species such as *P. lyallii* and *P. catarractae* can also be propagated from self-layered stems.

PARSONSIA (New Zealand jasmine)

SEED: Cool-moist stratify for 1–2 months before sowing and germinate in medium to warm conditions. Can be sown when fresh but germination takes up to 6 months. Seed ripens in February and March and it stores well.

CUTTINGS: Soft semi-hardwood cuttings taken in March and April are not difficult to root. Treat with hormone and root in cool to intermediate conditions. Rooting usually takes 2–5 months. Cuttings taken in October and November, when the plants are in flower, root quite successfully and enable selected clones to be propagated.

PASSIFLORA TETRANDRA (Kohia)

SEED: Sow when fresh and germinate in intermediate to warm conditions. Fruit usually ripens between March and May. Seed does not store well.

CUTTINGS: Soft semi-hardwood cuttings taken from February to April root quite readily. Treat with hormone and root in intermediate conditions. Male and female flowers are borne on separate plants and if the showy fruits are wanted both sexes must be propagated from cuttings.

PELLAEA

SPORES: Sow according to the technique described in chapter 2. Ripe sori can be collected at various times throughout the growing season.

DIVISION: *P. rotundifolia* and *P. falcata* are easily propagated by division, but I have not had a great deal of success with the Central Otago form of the as yet unnamed species, which is rather more difficult. Remove sections of rhizome containing several fronds and pot into a gritty spongy mix. Shorten the fronds so that a few pinnae are left on each frond. Keep in a cool shady place until new growth appears.

PENNANTIA

SEED: Sow when fresh. Germination occurs within about 2 months. One grower recommends scarifying the seed followed by cool-moist stratification for 1 month before sowing. Germinate in cool to intermediate conditions. Seed ripens between March and May and stores well.

CUTTINGS: The juvenile phase of these trees can be quite long-lasting. It also has male and female flowers on separate plants. The male flowers of *P. corymbosa* provide the best display so that it is desirable to propagate male plants from cuttings. Cutting-propagated plants also come into flower at a much younger age. Cuttings are not always easy to root. Semi-hardwood cuttings taken in February and March give the best results. Treat with hormone and root in intermediate conditions. Rooting can take quite a long time, e.g. up to 10 months for *P. baylisiana*.

PEPEROMIA URVILLEANA

SEED: Sow when fresh and germinate in warm conditions. Ripe seed can be collected throughout much of the year. Seed stores well.

DIVISION: Most easily propagated by division. Rooted pieces are very easily detached from the parent and should be potted into a humus-rich mix. Keep in shady but intermediate conditions until established. Softwood cuttings root very easily.

PERNETTYA

Some botanists now include this in the genus *Gaultheria*.

SEED: Cool-moist stratify for 2–3 months before sowing. Germinate in cool to intermediate conditions. Germination occurs within about 2 months. Fruits ripen between January and April. The seed stores well.

CUTTINGS: Soft to firm semi-hardwood cuttings taken during March and April root successfully. Treat with hormone. Root in cool to intermediate conditions.

DIVISION: Both *P. nana* and *P. alpina* can be divided quite easily. *P. macrostigma* is of straggly growth and it is not so easy to find suitable pieces for dividing, but sometimes self-layered stems can be removed from the parent and grown on.

PHEBALIUM NUDUM (Mairehau)

SEED: Sow when fresh and germinate in intermediate conditions. Seed usually ripens in December and January. It stores well.

CUTTINGS: Firm semi-hardwood cuttings should be taken during March and April. Sometimes, if conditions are unfavourable, they can be slow to root and the use of bottom heat can help to hasten rooting. Treat with hormone.

PHORMIUM (New Zealand flax)

SEED: Both species are easily raised from seed, and some selected clones (e.g. *P. cookianum* 'Green Dwarf') also come true from seed. Sow when fresh. Germination usually occurs within about 4 weeks or

so. If necessary, the seed can be cool-moist stored for several months before sowing at a more convenient time. Seed of *P. tenax* so stored for 5 months commenced germination within 12 days. In some districts damping off and collar rot can be a problem. Apparently the choice of parent plant for seed can have a strong influence on their incidence. If damping off appears use a suitable fungicide. Seed usually ripens between January and March and stores well.

DIVISION: All variegated and coloured-leaved cultivars, as well as clones that may not be true-breeding from seed, should be propagated by division. Apart from the sheer physical effort of digging up and dividing large plants, all phormiums propagate easily by division. It is much easier to divide younger plants before they become too large and unmanageable. Each fan of foliage provides one division. The leaves should be cut back severely, so that on larger-growing kinds they are about 40–60 cm long and on the smaller kinds 30–50 cm long. If the leaves are not cut back they wilt quite severely and can affect the well-being of the division. In addition, the floppy leaves are even more unsightly than those that have been cut back. New leaves soon make their appearance. Trim back the roots to about 15–20 cm long, but make sure they are long enough to help anchor the division into the ground. Divisions of the smaller kinds can be put into containers for growing on.

PHYLLACHNE

SEED: Cool-moist stratify for 2–3 months before sowing. Germinate in cool conditions. Seed usually ripens between February and April.

DIVISION: *Phyllachne* is easily divided providing the divisions are taken from the outside edge of the cushion. Pot into a gritty spongy mix and keep in cool shaded conditions until the they are well established.

PHYLLOCLADUS (Celery-leaved pine)

SEED: Cool-moist stratify for 3 months before sowing. Germination is probably erratic. Seed ripens in March and April and does not store well. Seed of *P. glaucus* is not always easy to obtain.

CUTTINGS: Semi-hardwood cuttings should be taken during March and April. Treat with hormone and root in cool to intermediate conditions. Wounding the bases of the cuttings could help with rooting. *P. aspleniifolius* var. *alpinus* is not too difficult from cuttings and is the main species propagated in this way. Glaucous-leaved clones of it are commonly cutting-propagated in Britain. *P. trichomanoides* is likely to be of similar difficulty and *P. glaucus* is probably quite difficult. Select only those shoots that have apical dominance for cuttings.

PHYMATOSORUS

SPORES: Sow according to the technique described in chapter 2. Ripe sori occur on plants over much of the growing season.

DIVISION: For *P. diversifolius*, sections of rhizome (preferably with a growing tip) should be cut off the parent plant and only lightly covered with some growing medium in a pot. It will need to be pegged down to hold it in place and the fronds should be shortened, leaving only the two lowest pinnae. Keep in a cool shady place until new growth appears. The terrestrial form of *P. scandens* is treated similarly, except that the fronds only need a slight shortening back. The climbing form of *P. scandens* can be grown in the same way, but looks better if grown in a vertical position so that its fronds can hang down. Pieces of rhizome should be pinned onto a slab of fern fibre or a similar background and have a little sphagnum moss packed around it to retain moisture. Keep in a cool shady place with a humid atmosphere until well established. Although not usually done, the climbing form of *P. diversifolius* can be treated in a similar manner.

PIMELEA

SEED: Cool-moist stratify for 3 months before sowing. Stratified seed takes 12–18 months to germinate. However, *P. tomentosa* seed germinates easily and within about 1–2 months. Seed sown in autumn when fresh can take up to 2 years to germinate. If the seed has been allowed to dry after harvesting, it should be scarified and then cool-moist stratified for 3 months before sowing. Some species have dry fruits whereas others are berry-like. The fruits ripen over varying periods; those of some species ripen between December and April, but seed of other species such as *P. longifolia*, *P. traversii* and *P. arenaria* ripens earlier between August and January.

CUTTINGS: Species such as *P. prostrata*, *P. urvilleana* and *P. longifolia* root fairly easily from soft semi-hardwood cuttings taken between January and April. Keep in intermediate conditions for rooting. Treat with hormone. One grower recommends softwood cuttings taken throughout the year. Some other species, particularly those with hairy foliage (*P. tomentosa*, *P. sericeovillosa* and *P. pulvinaris*), are very difficult from cuttings. Their hairy foliage attracts *Botrytis* like a magnet and is very difficult to control. Prostrate species such as *P. prostrata* and *P. urvilleana* can be propagated from self-rooted layers that often occur.

PISONIA BRUNONIANA (Parapara)

SEED: Sow when fresh and keep in warm conditions for germination. The large seeds should be sown individually. Seed ripens at various times throughout the growing season and does not store well. Handling and sowing the sticky seeds is easier if they are coated with some fine dry sand when they are harvested.

CUTTINGS: The two variegated cultivars can only be propagated from cuttings. Semi-hardwood cuttings are not difficult to root and can be taken any time that suitable material is available. Reduce the large leaves to about half their size. Treat with hormone. Bottom heat assists with quicker rooting, but they can also be rooted without.

PITTOSPORUM

SEED: All species can be raised from seed, but care must be taken that the parent plant is well isolated from other species with which it could hybridise, otherwise a mixed assemblage of hybrids could result. Some individual clones can be relatively true-breeding so that it is possible to propagate them from seed providing they are isolated from other clones.

As a general rule, *Pittosporum* seed should be cool-moist stratified for 2–3 months before sowing, but even then there is no guarantee that germination will occur relatively quickly or evenly. Germinate in cool to intermediate conditions. Seed sown when fresh can just as easily germinate within several months or 12 months, and can take up to 2 years. Seed of *P. tenuifolium* that had been dry stored for almost 4 months before sowing gave the following results: 1 seedling germinated after 5 months and then nothing more until the eighth month when virtually every seed germinated. Seed of *P. dallii* sown when fresh took over 12 months to germinate. *P. ralphii* seed has been known to take up to 4 years to germinate. *Pittosporum* seeds are covered with a very viscous substance which makes handling difficult. Some people advocate soaking the seeds in a weak solution of detergent, but I have found it is not very effective. The best way is the tried and proven method of mixing the seeds with a little dry sand. They are then much easier to handle and sow. One grower simply cuts the capsules in two with a pair of secateurs and sows everything. The resultant seedlings are pricked out soon after germination and before their roots become too entangled.

The ripening times for seed are quite variable. Some species, particularly the divaricating ones as well as *P.crassifolium*, *P. ralphii* and *P. eugenioides*, take 12 months or so for the seed to ripen. For the remainder, seed mainly ripens between January and April with a few ripening between October and December. The seed stores well.

CUTTINGS: Semi-hardwood cuttings can be taken at various times of the year when suitable material is available, with March and April being the optimum time. Treat with hormone and root in cool to intermediate conditions. Maintain a humid atmosphere around them at all times. Depending on the time of the year and the material used, rooting can take from about 6 weeks to 3 months. Variegated and other cultivars must be propagated from cuttings or, in some instances, they can be grafted.

GRAFTING: Cuttings of variegated cultivars of *P. ralphii* and *P. crassifolium* are not always easily rooted. Side grafting them onto seedling rootstocks of the appropriate species is possibly an easier way to propagate them. Refer to chapter 4 for details.

PLAGIANTHUS

SEED: Seed sown when fresh will germinate within 1–2 months. One grower recommends cool-moist stratification for 1 month before sowing. Seed ripens between January and March but needs to be collected when slightly green, otherwise it is soon attacked by a small grub. The seed stores well but should be dusted with an insecticide, such as Derris Dust, to prevent grubs from devouring it in storage.

CUTTINGS: Semi-hardwood or hardwood cuttings of *P. divaricatus* taken from February to April generally give the best results. Treat with hormone and root in cool conditions. Propagating *P. regius* from cuttings would eliminate the divaricating juvenile phase and also make it possible to propagate selected clones of the male tree, which has the more attractive flowers. So far softwood and semi-hardwood cuttings have failed. The best chance of success would probably be to try hardwood cuttings.

PLANCHONELLA COSTATA (Tawapou)

SEED: Sow seeds when fresh. Germinate in medium to warm conditions. It is not known how long they take to germinate. Seed ripens in about May and June and does not store well.

CUTTINGS: Nothing is known about its propagation from cuttings, but semi-hardwood cuttings should be possible.

PNEUMATOPTERIS PENNIGERA

SPORES: Sow according to the technique described in chapter 2. Ripe sori are usually to be found throughout most of the growing season.

POA

SEED: Seed can be sown when fresh or preferably after 1–2 months of dry storage. Either leave the seed uncovered or apply the merest suggestion of a covering. Germinate in well-lit cool to intermediate conditions and shade from direct sunlight. Germination usually occurs within about 10 days to 1 month. Depending on the species and locality, seed ripens between January and March. It stores well.

DIVISION: All are easily propagated by division and selected clones should only be propagated by this method. The foliage of divisions should be cut back to about half its length.

PODOCARPUS

SEED: Cool-moist stratify for 3–4 months before sowing. Germinate in cool to intermediate conditions. Germination can be erratic. Seed ripens in March and April and does not store well.

CUTTINGS: Semi-hardwood cuttings taken during March and April give the best results. Cuttings can also be taken at other times of the year whenever suitable material is available. Cuttings of *P. nivalis* taken during September root quite well. For *P. hallii* and *P. totara* it is preferable to select shoots that have apical dominance, but for *P. acutifolius* and *P. nivalis* it is not so important. Treat with hormone and root in cool to intermediate conditions. Depending on the time of year, rooting takes 2–8 months.

POLYSTICHUM

SPORES: Sow according to the technique described in chapter 2. Ripe sori of most species can be found throughout the growing season.

DIVISION: Smaller plants of all four species can be divided, providing they have formed more than one crown. The crowns are carefully separated so that each has some root attached. Cut back the fronds, leaving just a few pinnae at the base and pot into a gritty spongy mix. Keep in a cool shady position until new growth appears.

POMADERRIS

SEED: Sow when fresh and germinate in intermediate to warm conditions. Germination occurs within 2 months or less. Dry storage for 1–2 months before sowing could improve germination. Seed of most species usually ripens between November and January and it keeps well in storage. It falls quickly once the capsules ripen.

CUTTINGS: Semi-hardwood cuttings can be taken from February to April. Treat with hormone and root in intermediate conditions. Species such as *P. apetala* and *P. kumeraho* are generally propagated from seed, but some of the smaller-leaved species are frequently grown from cuttings.

PRATIA

SEED: Because all propagation of *Pratia* is by division, there is a lack of information concerning its seed propagation. Some forms of *Pratia* are unisexual and others are self-fertile. One grower records that seed cool-moist stratified for 2 months failed to germinate. One recommendation is to stratify the seed for 3 months before sowing. It is possible that dry storage for 2 months before sowing could be more effective in breaking dormancy. Germinate in cool to intermediate conditions. Ripe fruits of *P. angulata* can usually be harvested over many months, whereas the other species tend to have a more limited fruiting period.

DIVISION: This is the usual and easiest method of propagation. Divisions of suitable size are potted. A little shade for a few days until they are established is the only treatment they require.

PRUMNOPITYS (Matai and miro)

SEED: Both species are slow to germinate regardless of what treatment they are given. Miro (*P. ferruginea*) seeds are particularly slow and can take 3–5 years before germination commences. Some growers recommend cool-moist stratification for 2–12 months before sowing. Germination is erratic. Seed of *P. taxifolia* (matai) usually ripens during March and April and that of *P. ferruginea* a little later during May and June. Rats are fond of miro seed and often damage many seeds that fall to the ground, which makes harvesting difficult. The seed stores well.

CUTTINGS: Soft to firm semi-hardwood cuttings are not too difficult and, in particular, can be used for propagating the adult phase of *P. taxifolia*. March to April or August to October are suitable times for taking them. Treat with hormone and root in cool to intermediate conditions.

PSEUDOPANAX

SEED: Cool-moist stratify for 1–3 months before sowing. Germination usually occurs within 1–3 months. Seed sown when fresh can take almost 6 months to germinate. In some districts leaf spot can be a problem on the young seedlings. Use a suitable fungicide if it appears or as a preventive. Seed of most species ripens between January and April, but that of *P. arboreus* ripens from about September until February and with one or two species such as *P. chathamicus* and *P. lessonii* ripening tends to be between about April and July. The seed does not store well.

CUTTINGS: Soft to firm semi-hardwood cuttings taken during March and April give the best results. Treat with hormone and root in intermediate conditions. Species that have thick stems are more difficult from cuttings and it is necessary to search for smaller shoots that are not too thick. Cuttings of the adult phase of *P. edgerleyi* are also quite difficult.

PSEUDOWINTERA

SEED: Cool-moist stratify before sowing — one grower recommends 6 months. Germinate in cool conditions. Seed usually ripens between January and May and stores well.

CUTTINGS: Semi-hardwood cuttings taken during March and April give the best results. Treat with hormone and root in cool to intermediate conditions. Rooting can be quite slow and may take several months.

PTERIS

SPORES: Easily raised from spores, which should be sown according to the technique described in chapter 2. Ripe sori are usually to be found on plants throughout most of the growing season.

QUINTINIA

SEED: Cool-moist stratify for 1–2 months before sowing. Germinate in cool to medium conditions. Seed usually ripens between December and January.

CUTTINGS: Little is known concerning the cutting propagation of *Quintinia*, however as it belongs to the Escalloniaceae it should not be too difficult. Semi-hardwood cuttings taken during March and April should have a reasonable chance of success.

RANUNCULUS (Buttercups)

SEED: Cool-moist stratify for 2–3 months and sow from June to September. Germinate in cool to intermediate conditions. Germination usually occurs within 1–3 months. However, even with stratification, germination of *R. lyallii* seeds can take 12 months or more and may even germinate over 2–3 years. Seed of most species likely to be cultivated usually ripens between January and March. One or two earlier-flowering species ripen between October and December. The seed does not store well.

DIVISION: Most ranunculi can be propagated by division, preferably carried out in early spring before active growth commences. The crowns should be carefully separated from the parent plant, potted into a gritty spongy mix and kept in a cool shady place until established.

RAOULIA

SEED: Sow when fresh or dry store for 2 months before sowing. Alternatively, the seed of high-alpine species such as *R. eximia* can be cool-moist stratified for 2–3 months before sowing. Sow according to the scree technique described in chapter 2. Seed of most species ripens between January and March but *R. haastii* ripens as early as November. The high-alpine species mainly ripen between February and March. The seed does not store well.

DIVISION: All of the mat-forming species are easily propagated by division and this is the main method of propagation. Divisions are best taken off the outside edge of the mat so that they have a portion of the active growing edge. Pot them into a suitable medium and keep lightly shaded until they become established. The high-alpine species do not normally divide well.

RHABDOTHAMNUS SOLANDRI (Waiuatua)

SEED: Easily raised from seed, which can be sown when ripe or dry stored for 2 months before sowing. Germinate in intermediate or warm conditions. Ripe seed can usually be harvested at various times throughout the year. It stores well.

CUTTINGS: Soft semi-hardwood cuttings taken at any time suitable material is available are not difficult to root. Treat with hormone and root in intermediate to warm conditions. Cuttings taken during September and October give the best results. Selected clones and the yellow-flowered cultivar should be propagated only from cuttings.

RHOPALOSTYLIS SAPIDA (Nikau)

SEED: Sow when fresh. Seeds can be individually spaced in pots, trays or cell trays. Germinate in warm conditions. In cooler conditions germination can take up to 12 months. Fruits take almost 12 months to ripen and can be harvested throughout much of the year, particularly from February to November. Seed stores well.

RIPOGONUM SCANDENS (Supplejack)

SEED: Cool-moist stratify for 2–3 months before sowing. Germinate in intermediate to warm con-ditions. Ripe fruit can be harvested at various times throughout the year. The seeds do not store well.

RUMOHRA

SPORES: Sow according to the technique described in chapter 2. Ripe sori occur on plants throughout most of the growing season.

DIVISION: The rhizome can be divided, but the pieces are not easy to establish. It mainly grows as an epiphyte, especially on tree-fern trunks, but also grows terrestrially, particularly on humus mounds. Terrestrial forms are easier to divide with success. Cut

off short lengths of rhizome, each with 3–4 fronds and preferably a growing tip. Cut back the fronds to leave only the lowermost pinnae and pin the rhizome onto a humus-rich mix. Lightly cover with a little more of the mix and keep in a cool shady place with a humid atmosphere.

SAMOLUS REPENS (Maakoako)

SEED: Sow when fresh or dry store for 1–2 months before sowing. Germinate in intermediate conditions. Ripe seed can be harvested throughout much of the summer. The seed stores well.

DIVISION: This is the easiest and most convenient way of propagating this species. Pieces of any convenient size can be divided off the parent plant, put into pots and held until established.

SARCOCORNIA QUINQUEFLORA (Glasswort)

SEED: Dry store for 1–2 months before sowing. Germinate in intermediate conditions. Seed ripens between January and April, and it stores well.

DIVISION: As with *Samolus*, division is the usual method of propagation. Divide off suitable pieces, pot and stand in a sunny position until established.

SCANDIA ROSIFOLIA

SEED: Sow when fresh. Germination occurs within about 3–4 weeks. If the seed is a little old, soak in warm water for several hours before sowing. Seed usually ripens between November and February. It does not store well.

SCHEFFLERA DIGITATA (Pate)

SEED: Sow when fresh and germination occurs within about 2 months. Alternatively, cool-moist stratify for 1–2 months before sowing. Seed usually ripens between April and June and does not store well.

SCHIZEILEMA

SEED: Sow when fresh or dry store for 1–2 months before sowing. The seed of most species ripens between about December and March. It stores well.

DIVISION: All species are very easily divided. Remove divisions from the parent plant, put into pots and keep in a cool shady place until established.

SCHOENOPLECTUS VALIDUS (Kopupu, bulrush)

SEED: Can be propagated from seed, but division is the usual means. Sow when fresh and germinate in cool to intermediate conditions. Seed usually ripens between January and May. It stores well.

DIVISION: Easily divided. Divisions should be potted

and held until they are established. If a suitable wetland habitat is available they can be planted out directly.

SCLERANTHUS

SEED: *Scleranthus* species can be raised from seed, but division is the usual method of propagation. Dry store for 1–2 months before sowing and germinate in cool to intermediate conditions. Germination takes about 4–8 weeks. Seed usually ripens between January and April. It stores well.

DIVISION: The three species are very easily propagated by division. Cushions are divided into small pieces, often of just a few shoots, and potted individually or put into trays. Keep in a shady place for about 7–14 days or until they produce new growth.

SCUTELLARIA NOVAE-ZELANDIAE

SEED: Can be sown when fresh, but better if dry stored for about 1–2 months before sowing. Germinate in cool to intermediateconditions. Germination takes about 4 weeks. Seed ripens in February to March. It stores well.

DIVISION: Easily propagated by division of the creeping stems. Rooted pieces are cut from the parent plant, put into pots and the top growth trimmed back to prevent wilting. Keep in a cool shady place until new growth indicates they are established. It is also propagated from soft semi-hardwood cuttings.

SELLIERA RADICANS (Remu remu)

SEED: Sow when fresh or dry store for 2 months before sowing. Germinate in intermediate conditions. Seed ripens between January and April and it stores well.

DIVISION: Very easily propagated by division. Patches can be divided into as many pieces as required. The divisions are either potted or replanted directly into the garden.

SOLANUM (Poroporo)

SEED: Sow when fresh. Germinate in medium to warm conditions. Germination takes about 1–2 months. In warm localities ripe fruit can be harvested throughout much of the year, but in colder southern districts the fruits ripen mainly between January and May. The seed stores well.

CUTTINGS: Softwood and soft semi-hardwood cuttings can be taken any time that suitable material is available. Reduce the leaf area and root in warm conditions. Rooting takes about 2–6 weeks.

SOPHORA (Kowhai)

SEED: Sow slightly green seed when fresh. Older seed should be scarified, chipped or given hot-water treatment (77–90°C, soak for 48 hours). The method used by one nursery is to harvest the seed on 1 January or soon after, when the seed coat is still soft and green, and sow it immediately. This results in quick, high-percentage germination that saves a lot of time and effort. Germination of older seed given hot-water treatment can occur within 1–3 months, but if the treatment was not effective or the seed was very old, 12 months later it can still be sitting in the pot looking as good as when it was sown. One grower recommends scarifying the seed in sulphuric acid for 1 hour, or chipping the seed coat and soaking in water for 2–3 hours before sowing. Seed sown during winter often results in poor germination. *S. prostrata* appears to have a softer seed coat than the two other species and if giving it hot-water treatment, the water temperature should be only about 50°C. Seed ripens between January and March, but the seed pods often remain on the tree for quite some months afterwards, so that seed from the previous season's flowering can sometimes be harvested when the tree is in flower the following spring. The seed stores well.

CUTTINGS: Semi-hardwood cuttings taken from June to August give the best results. Cuttings should be taken from well-grown young plants. The basal ends of the cuttings should be wounded before treating with hormone (0.8% IBA). If bottom heat is used, rooting usually takes 6–10 weeks. Cutting propagation enables the juvenile phase to be by-passed and even small 1-year-old plants can flower.

STILBOCARPA

SEED: Sow when fresh or cool-moist stratify for 2–3 months before sowing. Germinate in cool conditions. Seed sown when fresh will probably not germinate until spring and germination will be erratic. Seed ripens from March to May and does not store well.

DIVISION: *S. lyallii* produces stolons that root into the ground to form new plants. They are easily detached for growing on. Old plants can be divided but it must be done carefully so as not to severely damage the whole plant.

STREBLUS

(syn. *Paratrophis*)

SEED: Seed can be sown when fresh, but germination is improved if it is cool-moist stratified for 1–3 months before sowing. Germinate in intermediate conditions. Fruit usually ripens between December and March but those of *S. smithii* ripen from June to October. The seed stores well.

CUTTINGS: Separate sexes, selected clones and *S. heterophyllus* 'Charles Devonshire' must be propagated from cuttings. Soft semi-hardwood cuttings taken during the summer, or firm semi-hardwood to hardwood cuttings taken from March to May give the best results. Treat with hormone and root in cool to intermediate conditions.

SWAINSONA NOVAE-ZELANDIAE

SEED: Cool-moist stratify for 2–3 months before sowing. Sow in a loose gritty mix. Germination takes about 2 months. Keep a careful watch for slugs and snails, which find the young seedlings particularly attractive. Seed ripens about February and it stores well.

DIVISION: Older plants can be divided if done carefully. The best time is in early spring just as growth is about to commence and plants need to be repotted. Divisions should be potted into a scree-type mix and kept moist, but not too wet, until new growth indicates that they are becoming established. They will then stand slightly more watering but they are still plants that require very good drainage.

SYZYGIUM MAIRE (Maire tawaka)

SEED: Sow when fresh and keep moist at all times to ensure the seed does not dry out. Germinate in cool to intermediate conditions. Seed ripens between about March and July. It does not store well.

CUTTINGS: Semi-hardwood cuttings taken in March and April give the best results. Treat with hormone and root in intermediate conditions.

TECOMANTHE SPECIOSA

SEED: Easily raised from seed, which should be sown when fresh and germinated in warm conditions. Seed ripens about March and does not store well.

CUTTINGS: Semi-hardwood cuttings are not too difficult to root. Treat with hormone and root in intermediate to warm conditions. Cuttings taken in October rooted within 3 months and gave the best results.

TEUCRIDIUM PARVIFOLIUM

SEED: Can be sown when fresh, but germination is improved if dry stored for 2–3 months before sowing. Germinate in intermediate conditions. Seed usually ripens between January and March. It stores well.

CUTTINGS: Semi-hardwood cuttings taken during March and April give the best results. Treat with hormone and root in cool to intermediate conditions.

TODEA BARBARA

SPORES: Sow according to the technique described in chapter 2. Ripe sori occur on plants throughout much of the growing season.

DIVISION: Clumps that have produced several crowns can be divided. After separating the divisions, put into pots and cut back the fronds so as to leave just one or two of the lowermost pinnae. Keep in a shady place until new growth appears.

TORONIA TORU (Toru)

SEED: Sow when fresh. Germination can take up to 2 years or more. Scarifying the seeds or giving them hot-water treatment could hasten germination. Germinate in cool to intermediate conditions. Seed usually ripens in February and March. It does not store well.

CUTTINGS: *Toronia* is usually propagated from seed, but there is no reason why cutting propagation should not be successful. Semi-hardwood cuttings taken during January and February would be worth trying. Wound the bases of the cuttings, treat with hormone and root in intermediate to warm conditions. Bottom heat could also assist rooting.

UNCINIA (Hook sedge, hook grass)

SEED: Sow when fresh or dry store for 1–2 months before sowing. Seed sown when fresh took 1 month to germinate, whereas stratified seed took 4 months. Germinate in cool to intermediate conditions. Seed ripens mainly from mid-summer to autumn. It stores well.

DIVISION: Clumps are easily divided. Cut back the foliage of divisions to about half its length, pot and keep in a shady place until new growth commences.

VIOLA

SEED: All three species are easily propagated from seed, which can be sown when fresh or dry stored and sown in the spring. Germinate in cool conditions. Seed usually ripens between December and March. It stores well.

DIVISION: *V. filicaulis* has creeping and rooting stems that form large patches and is very easily divided. Both *V. cunninghamii* and *V. lyallii* are tufted plants but can also be divided once they are large enough. Division can be carried out at almost any time during the growing season. Pot divisions and keep in a cool shady place until established.

VITEX LUCENS (Puriri)

SEED: Cool-moist stratify for 3 months before sowing in spring. Seed sown when fresh can take a long time to germinate. Germinate in intermediate to warm conditions. Seed ripens between February and September.

CUTTINGS: There is little information regarding propagating puriri from cuttings. Softwood cuttings taken from about January to March should have a reasonable chance of success, particularly if they are taken from good healthy shoots of young plants. Treat with hormone and root in warm conditions. The use of bottom heat could assist rooting.

WAHLENBERGIA

SEED: Sow when fresh or dry store for 2–3 months before sowing. The latter probably gives more even germination. Germinate in intermediate conditions. Normally germination will occur within about 4 weeks. Seed stratified for 1–2 months and sown in July and August took 1–3 months to germinate in cool conditions. Seed of some species usually ripens between about February and April. *W. gracilis* and *W. albomarginata* can flower over many months so that ripe seed can be harvested from about November to April. *W. cartilaginea* usually has a more limited flowering season with its seed ripening in March and April. The seed stores well.

DIVISION: With the exception of *W. gracilis* and *W. trichogyna*, both of which have a single taproot, all species can be propagated by division. Because of its specialised scree habitat *W. cartilaginea* can be a little more difficult, but cultivated plants are easier. It needs to be potted into a scree mix and only lightly shaded until established. Divisions of the other species should be carefully removed from the parent, potted into a free-draining mix and kept in cool lightly shaded conditions until established.

WEINMANNIA (Kamahi and towai)

SEED: Cool-moist stratify for 1 month before sowing. Germinate in intermediate conditions. Seed of *W. racemosa* ripens between January and March, and that of *W. silvicola* ripens between December and February. The seed is very quickly dispersed after ripening and harvesting must be carefully calculated. It has a limited storage life of perhaps 6 months.

CUTTINGS: Semi-hardwood cuttings taken from young plants between February and April are not too difficult to root. Treat with hormone and root in intermediate conditions.

XERONEMA CALLISTEMON (Poor Knights lily)

SEED: Sow when fresh. Germinate in intermediate to warm conditions. Germination can take up to 3 months depending on conditions. Once germination occurs it is necesary to keep the seedlings on the dry side and not over-water as they are easily attacked by *Phytophthora*. The seedlings are quite slow growing. Seed usually ripens between December and January and does not store well.

DIVISION: Older plants are easily propagated by division. Individual fans are removed making sure that each has some root attached. It is not usually necessary to reduce the length of the foliage because their rather succulent nature keeps them fairly turgid.

Pot the fans into a very free-draining mix and keep in intermediate to warm conditions until well established. Division should be carried out in the growing season, between about October and January, so that the divisions have time to make growth before winter.

Glossary

ADVENTITIOUS BUDS: growth buds that arise where they would not normally be expected.

ADVENTITIOUS ROOTS: roots that develop from stems or other tissue from which they would not normally arise.

AFTER-RIPENING: a term used to describe the biological changes occurring within the seeds of some plant species from the time the seed is shed until it germinates (usually some months later).

APEX (pl. apices): the tip of a stem; hence *apical bud*, the uppermost bud on a stem, and *apical shoot*, the uppermost stem on a system of branches.

APICAL BUD: see above.

APICAL DOMINANCE: when a terminal or apical bud inhibits the growth of lateral buds lower down the stem and so grows more rapidly than they do.

ARIL: an often pulpy appendage to a seed, usually as an outgrowth from the stalk of the ovule.

ASEXUAL PROPAGATION: propagation without the use of the plant's sexual reproductive organs; thus any vegetative method of propagation such as cuttings, grafting or division.

AXIL: the upper angle between a leaf or petiole and the stem to which it is attached.

CALLUS: corky tissue which forms naturally over a wound.

CAMBIUM: a layer of permanently meristematic cells in stems and roots from which the various conducting tissues develop.

CLONE: a genetically uniform assemblage of individuals derived originally from a single individual by asexual propagation.

COTYLEDON: a seed leaf; usually, but not always, the first to emerge above the ground on germination.

CROWN: the region at the junction of the root and the stem; usually in herbaceous plants and ferns.

CULTIVAR: any variety of plant or clone that owes its origin to horticulture through hybridisation, selection or mutation.

CURRENT YEAR'S GROWTH/WOOD: the shoots which have grown from buds during the present growing season.

DICOTYLEDON: any flowering plant belonging to the group Dicotyledonae. They have two embryonic seed leaves (or *cotyledons*) and true leaves with a net-like vein system.

DOMINANT: a gene or character producing the same phenotype, or external physical appearance, in a plant or part of a plant.

DORMANCY: the condition where viable seed fails to germinate when placed in conditions suitable for germination. It is caused be either external or internal factors which prevent the seed from germinating at the wrong time of the year. Hence *dormant*.

EMBRYO: those parts of a seed; the cotyledons, plumule, hypocotyl and radicle which collectively form the embryonic plant.

GENOTYPE: the particular combination of genes possessed by an individual plant.

GENUS (pl. genera): a group of closely related species that are presumed to have a common ancestry.

GRAFTING: propagation by uniting the shoot or single bud of one plant (the *scion*) with the root system and stem of another (the *stock* or *rootstock*).

HARDEN OFF: to acclimatise plants raised in warm conditions to cooler conditions.

HETEROZYGOUS: a plant in which sufficient number of genes on one chromosome differ from those on the other member of the chromosome pair. When self-pollinated there will be a certain amount of variation in the characteristics of the seedlings.

HOMOZYGOUS: a plant in which a high proportion of the genes on one chromosome are identical to those on the opposite member of the chromosome pair. Consequently the plant will breed relatively true from seed when self-pollinated.

HYBRID: a plant produced by the cross-pollination of two different plants. They are usually highly heterozygous.

INHIBITOR: a chemical that accumulates in fruit and seed-covering tissues during development and remains with the seed after harvest to inhibit germination.

LAYERING: propagation by inducing shoots to form roots while still attached to the parent plant.

LEACHING: the process of removing inhibitors from seeds by soaking them in running water or by frequently changing the water in a container.

MONOCOTYLEDON: any flowering plant of the Monocotyledonae. They have a single embryonic seed leaf (or *cotyledon*) with parallel veins and flowers with parts in multiples of threes.

MYCORRHIZA: an association of a fungus with a higher plant in which the fungus lives within or on the outside of the roots, thus forming a symbiotic relationship.

PAKIHI: open or barren land, especially flat, badly drained areas of the western part of the South Island with a characteristic vegetation of shrubby and rush-like plants.

PETIOLE: the stalk of a leaf.

pH: the degree of acidity or alkalinity. Below 7 on the pH scale is acidic; above 7 is alkaline.

PINNA (pl. pinnae). a leaflet or division, especially a primary division, of a pinnate leaf or frond.

PROPAGATION CASE: a box or similar structure in which seeds are germinated and cuttings rooted. It can have bottom heat or be unheated.

PROTHALLUS: a small flat green disc produced by a germinating fern spore and which bears the sexual reproductive organs that enable a new fern plant to develop.

RADICLE: the primitive root in a seed embryo, later becoming the first seedling root.

RHIZOME: an underground stem usually spreading more or less horizontally.

ROOTSTOCK: see grafting.

SCARIFICATION: the process of breaking, scratching, mechanically altering or softening the seed coats or coverings to make them permeable to water and gases.

SCION: see grafting.

SEED COAT: The tough protective layer surrounding a seed.

SPORANGIUM (pl. sporangia): a sac or other structure containing spores.

SPORE: a simple, asexual, usually single-celled reproductive body such as produced by ferns and related plants.

STIPES (pl. stipites): a term mainly used to refer to the petiolar part of a fern frond.

STOOL: a stemless mother plant from which shoots are produced, usually from below ground level. The shoots are frequently layered to produce new plants.

STRATIFICATION: a method of treating dormant seeds so that they are subjected to a period of chilling, or sometimes warming, to after-ripen the embryo.

SUFFRUTICOSE: refers to plants that are slightly woody at the base and with herbaceous shoots above.

TRANSPIRATION: the loss of water vapour from stems and leaves.

VARIETY: a distinct variant of a species; it may occur as a cultivated form (*cultivar*) or occur naturally as a botanical entity (*variety*).

Bibliography

Allan, H. H., *Flora of New Zealand*, vol. 1, Government Printer, Wellington,1970.

Bailey, L. M., *The Standard Cyclopedia of Horticulture*, MacMillan, New York, 1947.

Butcher, S. M. & Wood, S. M. N., 'The Vegetative Propagation of Sophora microphylla Ait.', in *Annual Journal* of Royal New Zealand Institute of Horticulture, No. 13, 52–54, 1985.

Cath, P. W., 'Propagation of *Nothofagus solandri* var. *cliffortioides* Vegetatively', in *New Zealand Journal of Forestry*, 17(2), 288–292,1972.

Chittenden, F. J. (ed.), *Dictionary of Gardening*, Oxford University Press, Oxford, 1951.

Dirr, M. A. & Heuser, C. W., *The Reference Manual of Woody Plant Propagation*, Varsity Press, Georgia, 1987.

Elliot, W. R. & Jones, D. L., *Encyclopaedia of Australian Plants Suitable for Cultivation*, vol. 1, Lothian Books, Melbourne, 1980.

Hammett, K., *Plant Propagation*, A. H. & A. W. Reed, Wellington, 1973.

Hartmann, H. T., Kester, D. E., & Davies, F. T., *Plant Propagation Principles and Practices*, 5th ed., Prentice Hall, New Jersey, 1990.

Kains, M. G. & McQuesten, L. M., *Propagation of Plants*, Orange Judd, New York, 1945.

MacDonald, B., *Practical Woody Plant Propagation*, vol. 1, Timber Press, Oregon, 1986.

Maloy, A., *Plants for Free*, Shoal Bay Press, Christπchurch, 1992.

Metcalf, L. J., *Cultivation of New Zealand Trees and Shrubs*, 5th ed., Reed, Auckland, 1991.

Metcalf, L. J., *The Cultivation of New Zealand Plants*, Godwit Press, Auckland, 1993.

Moore, L. B. & Edgar, E., *Flora of New Zealand*, vol. 2, Government Printer, Wellington, 1970.

Index

Note: For easier reference the common names of plants listed in the alphabetical section have been indexed. Scientific names have only been indexed where they occur in the first part of the text.